THE SOPHIA MYSTERY
IN OUR TIME

The Birth of Imagination

Mario Betti

TEMPLE LODGE

To my dear wife

Temple Lodge Publishing
Hillside House, The Square
Forest Row, RH18 5ES

www.templelodge.com

Published by Temple Lodge 1994
Reprinted 2013

Translated by Pauline Wehrle

Originally published in German under the title *Das Sophia-Mysterium der Gegenwart* by Verlag am Goetheanum, Dornach in 1992

© Philosophisch-Anthroposophischer Verlag am Goetheanum
This translation © Temple Lodge Publishing 1994

A catalogue record for this book is available from the British Library

ISBN 978 1 906999 50 6

Cover montage by Morgan Creative, featuring icon of Sophia, the Holy Wisdom (Russia 1812)
Typeset by DP Photosetting, Aylesbury, Bucks
Printed in the UK by 4edge Limited, Essex

Contents

WENN NICHT MEHR ZAHLEN UND FIGUREN
SIND SCHLÜSSEL ALLER KREATUREN,
WENN DIE, SO SINGEN ODER KÜSSEN,
MEHR ALS DIE TIEFGELEHRTEN WISSEN,
WENN SICH DIE WELT INS FREIE LEBEN,
UND IN DIE WELT WIRD ZURÜCK BEGEBEN,
WENN DANN SICH WIEDER LICHT UND SCHATTEN
ZU ECHTER KLARHEIT WERDEN GATTEN,
UND MAN IN MÄRCHEN UND GEDICHTEN
ERKENNT DIE EW'GEN WELTGESCHICHTEN,
DANN FLIEGT VOR *EINEM* GEHEIMEN WORT
DAS GANZE VERKEHRTE WESEN FORT.

Novalis

[When numbers and figures are no longer the key to all creatures,
When these will sing or kiss of more than the very learnèd know,
When the world returns to abundant life and life to the world,
When light and shadow pair up again with real clarity,
And people recognize the eternal truths in myths and poetry,
Then *one* secret word will drive away all distortion.]

Introduction

The real world surrounding us is many-layered and can only appear to us in the light in which we are capable of perceiving it. Whether we are materialists or spiritualists, idealists or pragmatists, reality will always show us the face which, in the words of Empedocles, proves that like can only understand like.

This makes every world view relative, yet what a multi-faceted world picture is then possible when we take the whole of humanity into account! In this sense the following ideas form no exception, for they are focused on one particular aspect of today's world situation.

In view of the world-encompassing nature of my theme these ideas will be incomplete in many ways, and therefore they are in no way intended to be the last word on the subject. They are meant solely as *pointers* to certain significant events that affect the inner core of everyone alive today and which up till now have received far too little attention. It is left to the reader to pursue these matters in greater depth if he or she so wishes.

This book is based on the work of many authors, above all on some of the fundamental results of the spiritual research of Rudolf Steiner. I refer to insights into the significance of the events of Golgotha at the turning point of time, and to the different parts of our human nature as a reincarnating spiritual individuality in their relation to a concrete world of spiritual beings and in their encounter with the powers of evil—with luciferic, ahrimanic and asuric beings.[1]

Nowadays we can all come to such insights through independent study, for they have their source in the true reality of the world and of humanity. In this sense the author wishes to assume full responsibility for this presentation, which touches in some places on new territory.

The confrontation with evil manifests as a battle taking place on many levels, the outcome of which lies in the hands of each one of us alive today. The most important requisite is the creating of a space within us in which a new consciousness, the Imagination, will gradually be able to arise. Much in the future depends on whether a sufficient number of people succeed in reaching this level of experience, where they will then be able to join with the good forces and beings active at this level— led by the Archangel Michael and Christ-Sophia— and thus help to bring civilization forward right into the nitty-gritty of practical life.

Experiencing Nature with Vision
Imaginative Consciousness

'... be it an idea, or be it life in the becoming?'

In the course of the last centuries and decades human consciousness has been undergoing a constant expansion, albeit a
one-sided one. Through the invention of the printing press and
by means of communication and information technologies, a
kind of global consciousness has arisen that puts us in a great
dilemma if we want really to be people of our time. On the one
hand we are inundated daily by a tremendous flood of information and on the other hand in a great many areas a kind of
specialization has arisen in which only a very small minority
can hope to get on top of. A level of knowledge that forms a
balance between these two extremes is becoming increasingly
necessary, to enable us to attain really soundly-based con-
ceptions about the world and human nature without our
succumbing to the superficiality of mere information or falling
victim to the one-sidedness of exaggerated specialization.
Greater and greater numbers of people are looking for the sort
of experience of the world such as we know of from the
lamentations of a despairing Faust:

> And thus the bitter task forego
> Of saying the things I do not know—
> That I may detect the inmost force
> Which binds the world and guides its course;
> Its germs, productive powers explore,
> And rummage in empty words no more![2]

Now it turns out that strengthened thinking and, even more
so, Imagination or imaginative consciousness, as Rudolf
Steiner calls the first stage of higher knowledge, puts us in a
position to be able to behold the forces actively at work in the
world and in human nature so that the resulting knowledge

can give rise to a comprehensive renewal and a new momentum in many areas of our culture, as anthroposophical spiritual science has been demonstrating for decades.[3] Rudolf Steiner has brought a first-ever training in this new method of knowledge out of the dim realm of future perspectives and described it as a task of our own particular cultural epoch, the so-called epoch of the consciousness soul or of the fifth post-Atlantean epoch which began in the fifteenth century AD and will continue until about the middle of the fourth millennium.[4]

> What special qualities are the people of the fifth post-Atlantean age, our own, to develop? We know that this is the age of the development of the consciousness soul and that, to accomplish this, a number of forces—soul and bodily forces—must be active. First a clear perception of the sense world is necessary, if human beings are to stay firmly on the Earth. This did not exist in earlier times because a visionary, imaginative element continuously played into the human soul. The Greeks still possessed fantasy ... The other task is to unfold free Imaginations side by side with the clear view of reality—in a way a kind of repetition of the Egypto-Chaldean age. To date humanity has not progressed too far in this task ... We must develop free Imaginations in which we move as freely as we do only in our intellect. That, then, is the other task of the fifth post-Atlantean age. The unfolding of these two faculties will lead to a right development of the consciousness soul in our present epoch.[5]

The evolution of natural science, particularly since Francis Bacon (1561–1626) and Galileo Galilei (1564–1642), does in fact show a tremendous change of direction towards the world of the senses which, from thence onwards, were to reveal their secrets solely through observation and experiment. In fact there seems to be something directly prophetic in the words of an impressive personality from the end of the Middle Ages, who was a passionate supporter of the method of experimentation. Roger Bacon (*c.* 1210–94) wrote:

> Another possibility are machines for navigation without row-

ers, so that large ships, suitable for both rivers and oceans, can be managed by a single pilot, and will travel at a greater speed than if they were full of people. Similarly, wagons can be made that travel at an inestimable speed without being drawn by a horse, such as our pictures of ancient battle chariots; and flying machines are possible with a man sitting in the middle turning some sort of device which sets artificial wings beating the air after the manner of a bird flying.[6]

Statements such as these were being written about two hundred years before Leonardo da Vinci (1452–1519).

This 'clear perception of the world of the senses' has now largely been acquired, and we can ask ourselves whether in our present age the Imagination, as the complement to this, is sufficiently developed. The following pages will be an attempt to answer this question.

What is in fact imaginative consciousness? The Latin *Imago* as good as means, among other things, picture or likeness. The word imagination is generally used to mean the ability to picture things. Rudolf Steiner uses it to refer to a supersensible perception that can assume a pictorial character. For a perception that is not sensory we have expressions like clairvoyance, or even ESP (extra sensory perception) as used in parapsychology and, more recently, in the New Age movement, yet the 'visions' and other experiences covered by these are so fundamentally different from Imaginations that it is essential we make a clear distinction between them.

In earlier times humanity had a dreamlike clairvoyance. An echo of this exists in the various folk myths and legends. That kind of vision was the expression of an instinctive connection with the whole cosmos, that is, with spiritual beings whose activities were experienced throughout nature. However, human beings were then not free. The deeper layers of their will were interconnected with the will of the gods in whose guidance they had implicit trust. This was in the pre-philosophical phase of humanity, way back in the so-called prehistoric age. Only vestiges of this survived over the centuries. The dreams of the pious Joseph, and of the three kings from the East, as described in St Matthew,[7] show clear echoes of this type of spiritual guidance, although we also find them in later times.

The course of human history shows a progressive liberation. From out of a pictorial, mythological consciousness, as from a maternal womb, there slowly came forth a discursive, abstract thinking that was directed more and more towards the outer phenomena of nature. Visionary perception was bound to disappear if human beings were to learn to take on their own responsibility for their thinking and actions, and do so in a state of wide-awake consciousness. Where scholars of science and philosophy are concerned we find an indication of a kind of world-historic conclusion of visionary consciousness in the transition from the kind of thinking of the teachers of the famous School of Chartres, which was chiefly of a pictorial, allegorical character, to the more conceptual thinking of the great Scholastics who introduced modern consciousness.[8] The change-over was around the year 1250.[9]

A significant individual of the thirteenth century, a cultured scholar and diplomat, Brunetto Latini (c. 1220–94), who later on was the teacher of Dante Alighieri, became capable under special circumstances of seeing into those supersensible worlds whence come the creative forces that fashion both the human realm and nature. His testimony is so important for our theme that a lengthy quotation from his *Tesoretto* shall be included here. It is ascribed to the year 1260. After the Battle of Montaperti the Guelph party loyal to the Pope in Florence had to yield up its power. Brunetto Latini, too, on an important mission with King Alfonso X of Castile, was on the list of exiles. When on the return journey he reached Roncesvalles, and received the news from a wandering Bolognese scholar that Florence had fallen into the hands of the opposing side and that he could not return, he was overcome by grief and lost his way:

> Continuing my way with a bowed head

sunk in thought and full of sorrow
I left the main road and going along wrong paths
came to a strange forest.
Returning to consciousness I looked around
and directed my gaze to the encircling mountains;
and I saw a great crowd of different sorts of animals,
I know not rightly of what kind they were.
There were males and females,
Cattle, snakes and beasts of prey,
a great multitude of fish
and many kinds of flying birds.
I also saw plants, fruits and flowers,
jewels and pearls that are highly prized,
and so many other things
that nobody could find words
to name or to distinguish them.
I can say only one thing:
I saw them all
from the aspect of their end and their beginning,
their dying and their coming into being
and their assuming the character of their species
at the behest of a figure whom I beheld.
Sometimes she appeared to be embodied
and sometimes quite formless.
Often she touched the sky
as though it were her mantle,
and sometimes she transformed it.
The skies moved according to her command.
She often expanded
so that she appeared to hold
the whole world in her arms.
She sometimes laughed and
sometimes her features showed pain and anger,
until her face radiated again like the sun...

I will say only so much as that
her hair was wonderful,
like fine gold,
parted and without plaits.

Every part of her face was beautiful,
beneath a white brow...

I must refrain from further description,
not because of the trouble it would cost me,
nor because of faintheartedness,
but because it is not possible
either by word of mouth nor with the pen
to describe her beauty fully,
nor her activity in the air,
on the earth or in the sea,
creating and undoing
and creating again anew,
be it an idea, or be it life in the becoming
or a different form of primal beginning—
all in accordance with their image.
I saw that it was through her rulership
that every creature that has a beginning
also arrives at its end.
Then, seeing me,
she turned her smiling face towards me
and taking me into her secret confidence
said: 'I am *Natura*...'[10]

Then the astonished scholar was entrusted with important secrets of creation, and Natura also proved capable of leading him into the depths of his soul. By the end of this poem, which amounts to almost three thousand verses, and yet is only a fragment, Brunetto Latini had become a different person. The impact of this journey of the soul brought him profound world-knowledge and self-knowledge.

We can sense here in every direction the signs of genuine spiritual experience. We are struck by the sensory-anthropomorphic nature of this vision that was characteristic of atavistic clairvoyance, and the tremendous dynamic of the whole scenario: end—beginning; dying—coming into being; embodied—formless; expansion—contraction; everything in constant movement and change. We are reminded here of

Goethe's poetic version of the metamorphosis of plants, especially of the introductory framework poem 'Parabase':

> Freudig war vor vielen Jahren
> Eifrig so der Geist bestrebt,
> Zu erforschen, zu erfahren,
> Wie Natur im Schaffen lebt.
> Und es ist das ewig Eine,
> Das sich vielfach offenbart;
> Klein das Grosse, gross das Kleine,
> Alles nach der eignen Art.
> Immer wechselnd, fest sich haltend
> Nah und fern und fern und nah;
> So gestaltend, umgestaltend—
> Zum Erstaunen bin ich da.

> (Many years ago my mind was eagerly and joyfully
> on a search to discover and experience
> how nature does its creating.
> and it is eternally one and the same thing
> revealing itself in countless ways;
> The big becomes small, the small big,
> each in its own way.
> Always changing, always remaining itself,
> near and far and far and near;
> forever forming and reforming—
> and I am here to wonder at it all.)

Yet in Goethe's case he does not have a visionary bent and he brings his findings in the clear light of self-acquired knowledge. It took Goethe many years of observing and researching to work his way through to the comprehensive world view we find in his natural scientific works. The centuries that followed Brunetto Latini witnessed the advent of a deeply justified but one-sidedly materialistic natural science. The advancing emancipation from the divine basis of the world was a gigantic process of contraction. The light aura of a cosmically orientated consciousness sank into the depths of the human soul. Human beings began to think for themselves, thus achieving a significant step in inner independence. Their estrangement from the spirit had to go so far that human beings were bound to deny the very existence of anything supersensible. Goethe's 'intuitive power of judgement' in contradistinction to Kant's 'discursive power of judgement' was supposed to inaugurate a new epoch of spiritually aware scientific research, an epoch given to a holistic understanding of life. But in the final resort it all remained an episode hardly taken seriously by materialistic natural science. Due to his rigorous phenomenalism, coupled with a genuine artistic nature, Goethe possessed the ideal qualities for developing a new consciousness the signs of which we see in his 'archetypal plant' and in parts of his *Faust*. But it went no further than a few beginnings. This was also connected with the fact that although he was able to enter with objectivity into the world of phenomena he had slight regard for the foundation of all knowledge, without the strengthening of which no holistic knowledge capable of grasping both a lower and a higher reality would in the long run be possible, namely, thinking. Rudolf Steiner, who recognized in Goethe the 'Copernicus and Kepler of the organic world'[11] carried on where Goethe left off and systematically built up spiritual science, anthroposophy, as 'a path of knowledge capable of leading us in the spiritual part of our human nature to the spirit in the cosmos'.[12] He points time and again to the importance of thinking for acquiring a spiritual consciousness. As an example:

> ... for all of you have a tiny amount of clairvoyance. And what is this that we all have? It is something not generally appreciated to be clairvoyance ... No one could think abstractly, could really have thoughts and ideas, if they were not clairvoyant, for from the start the pearl of clairvoyance has been in our ordinary thoughts and ideas. These thoughts and ideas arise in the soul through exactly the same process as that which gives rise to its highest powers. It is tremendously important

that we learn to understand in the first place that clairvoyance begins in something of quite an everyday nature: we must only grasp *the supersensible nature of concepts and ideas.* We must realize that it is from supersensible worlds that concepts and ideas come to us, for only then shall we see things correctly. When I talk to you about the higher Hierarchies, about the Seraphim, Cherubim and Thrones down to the Archangels and Angels, those are Beings who have to speak to the human soul from higher, spiritual worlds. It is from these same worlds that ideas and concepts come to our souls. They come directly from higher worlds and not from the world of the senses.

It was held to be a significant statement by a significant figure of the Enlightenment when people were told in the eighteenth century: Fellow humans, have the courage to make use of your power of reason.—Today an even more important statement must be heard in the soul, saying: Fellow humans, have the courage to treat your concepts and ideas as the starting point of your clairvoyance.—What I have just expressed I said many years ago publicly in my books *Truth and Science* and *The Philosophy of Freedom* where I showed that human ideas come from a supersensible, spiritual knowing.[13]

This, then, is one particular path of training on which a person, while losing nothing of his or her inner freedom and full wakefulness, can attain a modern form of 'clairvoyance', namely, Imagination.

Human consciousness is capable of receiving images on many levels. By way of example let us review some phenomena which are, however, not in every instance completely distinct from one another:

mental images
memories
dreams
visions
hallucinations
fantasy
imagination

Mental images are the pictures we make of our perceptions. They are the pictures that 'stick' when we engage our senses and bring the diversified impressions of these to consciousness through our thinking. The table in front of us, the flower by the wayside, the rustling sound nearby: all these are formed in us into mental images, though this takes place so fast that we are totally unaware of how it happens.

Our memory can take hold of perceptions that have sunk into our unconscious and fill them out again as pictures or sounds. Having now become mental images they can be of service to our thinking. The whole range of our sense impressions can be thus recaptured anew. Each memory is fresh each time, even though the perception belongs way back in the past.

It is just this picture-creating ability of the soul that, giving us as it does faithful replicas of our impressions, enables us altogether to have a continuous, conscious soul life. If you try to remember exactly what an acquaintance looked like whom you saw a short while ago you may notice, even though we are usually unconscious of it, what a musical, sculptural, pictorial quality can be attributed to memory. One particular detail, one particular colour, will often be given quite a different nuance, and this helps us realize that we are not merely fishing out the same old impression. Also, as each of you will be able to observe for yourselves, the picture quality of our memories alters in the course of the years and the decades. Hermann Poppelbaum says the following about the dynamic process of memory: 'A naive conception of memory thinks of it as some sort of file index in the soul, where we only need to pick out the correct picture from a large storage bin and lift it to the light. But recollection is a creative deed, a re-imagining, not a simple act of picking up. Something is repictured which before this had ceased to be a picture. The intangible becomes tangible again.'[14]

The criterion for judging the veracity of memory is of course the accuracy with which it reproduces past experiences. This is no longer the case at all at the next level, that of dream, as now the artistic power of picture-making goes entirely its own way. Experiences from long ago, from bodily and soul depths, from heights of the spirit, everything can be included in a dream and turned into pictures or sounds. There is good reason for using dreams as significant pointers in the labyrinth of the psyche.

Visions that we know of from the lives of many saints and also in the impressive experience of Brunetto Latini are no exception in this series in so far as their image character shows the typical anthropomorphic and, as a rule, instinctive quality of a dream. In certain circumstances we can also speak of waking dreams. But ordinary dreams are mainly subjective. True visions can give signs of things invisibly at work both within the human being and nature. It is not the image as such that is the spiritual reality—just as little as it is with Imaginations—but *what the image represents*. We must always bear in mind that it is our own soul that produces the pictures, and it is from the whole reservoir of all our various memories that we pick the raw material that appears in all manner of variations in visions. Experiences from this quarter, though they are not desirable these days because now is the time for a different level of consciousness, are of no clinical relevance so long as the 'seer' is conscious of their visionary character and is not overwhelmed by them.

The matter is different in the case of so-called optical or acoustic illusions, i.e. hallucinations that signify a pathological, unconscious projection of soul or bodily processes into the perceptual world. The effects of so-called hallucinogens also belong here.

Fantasy is where the artistic, picture-making force of the soul comes to most free expression. Here the ego can lord it and produce the most weird and wonderful things. This is the force that is perpetually bringing new creations into our world and which, among other things, is responsible for the picture-making ability we have already mentioned.

Yet however varied and colourful, grand and sublime these dreams, visions and fantasies may be—to think of C.G. Jung[15]—they are all in a certain respect 'bodybound' in so far as in the last resort they all arise out of the almost inexhaustible treasure of all our stored-up earthly experiences. Lucid dreams are no exception.[16]

All these phenomena, however transparent they may be, are always tied up with sense perceptions, and even if subtle beyond recognition they are the expression of the human bodily constitution and its formative forces that are also connected with the soul—as was likewise the case with the atavistic clairvoyance of olden times.

It is quite a different story when we come to Imaginations that are produced in freedom, and which, as already mentioned, are the only kind that are significant for our time. Imagination also creates its pictures with soul material. It also has different levels of transparency and intensity according to the aptitude and maturity of the individual concerned. To start with it can have a kind of memory character, such as fleeting impressions or something similar to waking dreams. However, real, fully developed Imagination is capable of becoming a genuine *body-free*, supersensible experience that can grasp the true nature of the human being and the natural world. Just as with the ordinary acquisition of knowledge there has to be an object to see and know, there also has to be one in the case of pure, supersensible perception—only this 'perceiving' is an incomparably more dynamic process. Experience shows that the 'eye' of Imagination does not function automatically in the sense that our physical eyes do but that it has to be creatively active where each new perception is concerned. This organ of perception is not constructed of bodily substance. In the forefront of imaginative experience—which becomes ever less anthropomorphic—the soul sends out its substance by way of the greatest inner activity towards a spiritual entity which clothes itself in this soul substance in order to make itself manifest. The knowing subject and the known object to a certain degree merge together.

As already indicated, the Imaginations themselves are solely indications, footprints as it were, of the respective spiritual beings who use the pictures arising in this way as letters of a purely spiritual language. Sometimes it happens in the case of great works of art that the power of fantasy itself reaches the imaginative sphere, thus becoming 'exact' fantasy. In this instance it towers above the artist's own subjective soul realm, revealing some glimpses of the objective spiritual cosmos in and around us. In real works of art, subject and object merge together.

Rudolf Steiner calls the study of spiritual science the beginning of this new path to an expanded consciousness. In the course of this study thinking can become enlivened from within, and out of this new beginning there then arise the higher possibilities of knowledge called in anthroposophy Imagination, Inspiration and Intuition.[17] Although the *emphasis* in this book is on *imaginative consciousness* it is important to know that these three stages are as it were intertwined. When one of them sounds the others resound in sympathy. Rudolf Steiner once formulated this fact thus: 'What is seen and experienced in the spirit can only be conveyed in picture-form, that is, in Imaginations through which Inspirations speak which in their turn proceed from spiritual reality of being experienced in Intuition.'[18] That this is so is connected with the inner qualities of thoughts. We have already referred to the picture character of mental images. Behind each mental image there is a particular concept, like a common denominator, the homogeneous originator of all the possible mental images. By way of example, there are many beds but only one idea 'bed'—as Plato explains so impressively in his *Republic*—and it must not be thought of as a finished bed but as a pictureless concept. This idea is the prototype of all possible beds. On the basis of this one idea 'bed' artists or joiners can imagine and produce any amount of different kinds of beds.

Or think of a square. There are innumerable possible squares—that is to say mental images—but only one concept 'square', which must not be thought of pictorially but described in words: a square is a quadrangle with four sides of equal length and four right angles. This description does not restrict it to one particular image.

The description of a concept is at the same time its explanation. By thinking it through I immediately understand the meaning of the concept. This understanding purely by means of the concept or the conceptual complex goes beyond merely seeing it as a mental image. It is a statement that sheds light on the respective concept from within, thus including all the possible mental images of it. You are becoming aware here of the pure light of consciousness, even if you are concentrating on an absolutely commonplace thought. If you now intensify your concentration, you can experience this meaning, this statement—this inner word—as the expression of a quite definite force that is dynamically creative in the extreme and with which you can unite, and this force manifests as a quite definite concrete spiritual being: the being of the respective idea.

This may sound very strange in the first instance, yet these are experiences anyone can have in the course of inner training, in meditation.

There are, then, these three elements: a mental image, a concept as a higher principle, and an empirical force of being as its innermost core. These elements can be discovered in every commonplace thought. As a rule we get our mental images and concepts from the surrounding world or in reflecting on a memory. Imagination means getting mental images from concepts which do not arise in the world of perception. These concepts, which literally unveil themselves as spiritual beings in our inner experience, are directly 'intelligible'. One understands their language. As such these concepts are already the

Inspirations with which we can understand the imaginative pictures. If inner experience is intensified a stage further it is possible to experience in Intuition a kind of union with the respective spiritual being. One grows into this being, who can be recognized in full wakefulness as a higher reality.

Ordinary thinking happens as it were automatically. This more intensive thinking, which is incomparably more dynamic, can only be created if it is willed.

We discover here the answer to a question that arises at a certain level of knowledge: are Imaginations, Inspirations and Intuitions revelations from outside or are they solely human creations?

They are both.

It is generally speaking my intense inner activity that makes possible the imaginative revelation of a spiritual being. The awakening of Inspiration, as it were, the interpretation of the respective image, is also the result of inner creativity, and in Intuition this inner creativity reaches an undreamt of intensity. However contradictory this sounds, these are at one and the same time manifestations of the self and of the world taking place in full wakefulness. These are not visions, nor are they 'messages' from the so-called Beyond, for the ego is fully present. Everything else—which is almost all one hears about nowadays—is more or less obvious cases of possession, even when the messages are received and passed on with the best intentions. We shall go into this aspect in greater detail in a later chapter. Rudolf Steiner himself says the following about the dynamics of this higher knowledge:

> You experience total freedom with regard to place and time, you feel in motion. Certain linear forms and shapes are experienced, yet you do not experience them as though you saw them drawn in some kind of space but as though in continuous movement every single curve, every form, was followed by the ego. In fact the ego is felt at one and the same time as the draughtsman and the drawing material. Every linear direction, every shift in position, is an experience of this ego. You

recognize that with your moving ego you are bound up with the world's creative forces. The universal laws are no longer something that the ego perceives outwardly but a truly miraculous fabric that it is helping to weave. Occult science designs all kinds of symbolic drawings and pictures. When these really correspond to fact and are not mere invented figures they are based on the observer's experience in higher worlds which are to be viewed as described above.

This is how the world of Inspiration is placed within the imaginative world. When Imaginations begin to disclose their meaning to the seer in 'silent speech' then the world of Inspiration arises *within* the imaginative world.[19]

Rudolf Steiner calls the world in which Imaginations arise and are active not only the world of Imagination but also the astral or the elemental world. The worlds of Inspiration and Intuition which constantly interpenetrate the imaginative sphere belong to higher realms of the spiritual world.[20]

The processes of consciousness taking place in Imagination are very subtle ones. They have no trace of anything tumultuous or sensational in the ordinary sense as dreams or visions so often have. An indispensable factor here is that you have to have thorough self-knowledge, right into your deepest depths. For the first supersensible reality you have dealings with is usually your own soul, and you must have acquired a certain degree of clarity in this area if you do not want to find yourself all the time succumbing to illusions from your unconscious soul life.

A path of knowledge of this kind is a path of inner transformation which, proceeding from thinking, gradually passes over to one's whole being. A gentle but all the more powerful 'dying and becoming' is always part of such a path. A person undergoing this training must increasingly get rid of old habits of thought and customary feelings of self-esteem in order to reach the real threshold of Imagination, which is actually the threshold of the spiritual world itself. The illusion that thoughts are *mere* thoughts must be thoroughly overcome.

A modern person who, for the most part, only believes in outer reality may not find this first step easy. It is a matter of taking the thought world seriously and gradually grasping the fact it is the first manifestation of a purely spiritual world, even if it is shadowy to start with. It is only on this foundation that the full light of imaginative consciousness can slowly arise. Then a progressive process of objectification takes place whereby not only Imaginations on the level of self but also cosmic Imaginations are possible. By means of Imagination, which is of course developed alongside normal waking consciousness, extensive areas of both the earthly and the spiritual world and their creative interrelationship can be researched. The boundaries of the imaginative plane are flowing and in perpetual movement:

> Something existing in the physical world takes place differently in the imaginative world. In the former we see a continuous arising and decaying, an alternation between birth and death. In place of this phenomenon there occurs in the imaginative world a perpetual *transformation* of one state into another. For instance in the physical world you see a plant *decaying*. In the imaginative world you see, as the plant withers, another structure arising, not physically perceptible, and into which the withering plant is gradually changing. When the plant has completely disappeared the structure is then fully developed in its place. Birth and death are mental images that lose their meaning in the imaginative world. In their place there is the concept of *transformation of one thing into another*. Because this is so it is possible for imaginative knowing to approach the particular truths about the human constitution that appear in this book [*Occult Science*] in the chapter 'The Nature of Humanity'. Physical sensory perception can see only the processes of the physical body. They take place in the 'realm of birth and death'. The other members of the human being, life body, sentient body and ego, are subject to the laws of transformation, and they can be perceived by imaginative knowledge. Someone who has progressed to this level can perceive at

death something as it were released from the physical body that
then lives on in another form of existence.[21]

Not only temporal dimensions but also spatial dimensions
are different here:

> For space in the imaginative world is not at all like it is in the
> physical. Whoever fancies that he has imaginative colour
> pictures in front of him when he is seeing freely floating
> coloured particles in ordinary space dimension is in error. But
> the forming of such colour representations is, nevertheless, the
> *way* to imaginative life. Whoever tries to put a flower before his
> mind's eye and then separates off from his picture everything
> that does not represent colour, so that an image of the coloured
> surface, separate from the flower, hovers before his soul, can
> *gradually* through such exercises *arrive* at an Imagination. This
> picture itself is not yet such an Imagination but is more or less a
> preliminary fantasy suggestion. Imagination, that is, the real
> astral experience, exists for the first time when not only the
> colour is wholly separated from the sense impression but when
> also three-dimensional space has been totally discarded. That
> this is the case can be confirmed only by a certain feeling. One
> can only describe this feeling by saying that one no longer feels
> outside but *inside* the colour-picture and one is conscious of
> partaking in its coming into being. If this feeling is not there, if
> one remains standing before the thing as before a sense-bound
> colour-picture, then one is not dealing with a real Imagination
> but with something fanciful.[22]

In *Knowledge of the Higher Worlds: How is it Achieved?*, a
book of fundamental importance for the development of one's
own imaginative faculty, Rudolf Steiner says the following
about these things, and in a later place describes the new
clairvoyance as the movement of organs of higher perception,
the 'lotus flowers':

> It must be explicitly emphasized that the colours here described
> are not seen as the physical eye sees colours, but that through
> spiritual perception the same feeling is experienced as in the
> case of a physical colour impression. To apprehend blue

spiritually means to have a sensation similar to the one experienced when the physical eye rests on the colour blue. This fact must be noted by all who intend to rise to spiritual perception. Otherwise they will expect a mere repetition of the physical in the spiritual. This could only lead to the bitterest deception.[23]

However, we must not form too narrow a concept of spiritual 'vision'

for in that world there are not mére light and colour perceptions comparable to the experience of sight in the physical world but also impressions of heat and cold, taste and smell, and still other experiences of the imaginative 'senses' for which the physical world offers no likeness. Impressions of heat and cold are, in the imaginative (astral) world, revelations of will and intention of soul and spirit beings. Whether such a being aims for good or evil comes to light in a definite effect of heat or cold. Astral beings can also be 'tasted' or 'smelled'.[24]

From these few passages alone, that for their importance's sake have been quoted at length, you will see what breadth there is to imaginative experience. From the point of view of humanity as a whole a total mastery of these capacities is still a distant aim, yet what is to blossom later has to be sown today.

Indeed there are a number of significant aspects with regard to imaginative consciousness: the aspect of the individual, of social life and of the Earth. From a wealth of possible examples let me choose three that have a direct bearing on statements made in this connection by Rudolf Steiner, who was the first to speak about these things in unmistakable clarity.

Beside the regenerating forces gained from the acquisition of new insights the individual who, step by step, develops the ability to have Imaginations acquires a store of active forces containing a thoroughgoing healing force that is part of those areas of a person's life forces that Rudolf Steiner calls the etheric body, and which are primarily responsible for the growth, development and sustaining of our various organs:

Imaginative knowledge works down into the etheric body and from there into the blood, and this is the mediator which acts formatively on the organism. Human beings will become increasingly more able to work on their organisms through the etheric body. All imaginative knowledge based on truth is at the same time healing and health-giving; it makes the blood healthy in its circulation.[25]

The following perspectives apply to the social life:

It is only in images, in Imaginations, that the social life can be rightly established in the future. By means of abstractions the social life could be regulated only as regards a single people, and the regulation for one nation in social relationships was that of the Old Testament. The next form of regulation of the social life will depend upon the capacity to exercise in a conscious way the same force that once existed atavistically in unconscious or half-conscious form in the capacity to create myths. Human beings would be completely filled with anti-social instincts if they were to endeavour to remain at the stage of disseminating mere abstract laws. We must come again by way of our world conception to the pictorial element. Out of this conscious myth creation there will arise also the possibility for the development of the social element in the relationship of one person to another.

You may look at such a sculptural form as that of our 'Group'[26] (see illustration): the Representative of Man, Lucifer and Ahriman. There you confront for the first time what is working in the whole human being, because our true nature is a state of balance between the luciferic and the ahrimanic elements. If you permeate yourself in actual life with the impulse to confront every person in such a way that you see this trinity in him or her, then you begin to understand them. This is an essential capacity bearing within itself the impulse to evolve in this fifth post-Atlantean epoch ... What is raying out from the innermost part of human nature, striving towards realization, is that when one individual confronts another a picture shall come forth from the other person, a picture of that special form of balance manifested individually by everyone.

The 'Group' (The Representative of Man, Lucifer, and Ahriman)

... This capacity to be mystically stimulated as we confront another person will come to realization. It will enter in the form of a special social impulse into human life. On the one hand the consciousness soul is striving to come in an antisocial way to complete fruition in this fifth post-Atlantean epoch. On the other hand something else is striving outward from human nature, namely, the capacity to form pictures of the human beings with whom we live or whom we encounter in life. It is here that the social impulses arise, the social instincts. The simple fact is that these things lie at a far greater depth than is ordinarily supposed when people talk about what is social and what is antisocial.

... It is precisely in our social life that the principle must come into existence: Thou shalt make for thyself an image of thy fellow human being ... then when we form a picture of our fellow human beings we shall enrich our own soul life; we bestow a treasure upon our own inner soul life with each human acquaintanceship ... We acquire the capacity to have other human beings live in us.[27]

This picture we have just quoted arises out of experiencing the human being holistically, and it can be done in ordinary daily life. It is a matter of condensing certain impressions into a picture. Here is a brief indication of what is meant. We shall return to this trinity in a later chapter.

The luciferic element represents all that comes under the heading of egoism, self-indulgence in all its forms and also estrangement and escape from the world. Self-centred mysticism belongs here. All this represents a power that wants to raise a person above his fellows, pulling him so to speak 'upwards'. In the picture given us in the New Testament of the temptations of Jesus after the Baptism in the Jordan, it is the being who leads Him to the top of the mountain and offers Him world rule.

The other element, the ahrimanic one, represents the opposite. This is a kind of addiction to the world, where the solution to all problems is seen in the acquisition of material goods. This is portrayed in the picture of the temptation to turn stones into bread, disregarding the fact that as spiritual beings humans cannot live by bread alone. This power denies the spirit in both humanity and the cosmos. It is a power that pulls us as it were 'downwards' to mere matter, to death in fact. It is active in dead, abstract intellectualism and in hopeless pessimism with regard to the world and humanity.

These are the powers that occupy large areas of our soul and which we notice especially strongly at work in other people. There are, however, not only two aspects of human nature, for in each person there lives a 'golden' centre, which we often have to search hard for, because it is not so obvious as the two extremes. This meditation leads us gradually to experience human nature more and more comprehensively in a manner that can produce substance for practical social application. It helps us find and cultivate that really human centre where the true representative of humanity, the Christ, can so to speak put the two opposites into their right place, for the very way we regard our fellow human beings has its effect upon them. With the helping strength of the Christ selfish wilfulness and escapism become ego-respecting devotion to the world and its needs. The rigidifying tendencies of Ahriman in all their forms can become the firm backbone of our egohood on Earth. For even though the physical-material aspect of this represents the ground upon which the spiritual-cultural development of mankind advances, from the spiritual point of view the Christ points the way to a new beginning. The Representative of Mankind can make us gradually into 'balanced' people, and our awakening Imagination gives us an entry into the creative middle sphere.

And finally, where the future evolution of the Earth is concerned, the imaginative consciousness is of immeasurable importance. Imaginations as concrete spiritual creations are building stones of a cosmos in the becoming:

For into the general intellectual consciousness of humanity

there will gradually enter the power of Imagination ... By means of their Imaginations, however, human beings reach up into a higher spiritual world, similarly to the way they reach in memory into their own human nature. Human beings do not keep their Imaginations in themselves; they are inscribed into cosmic existence.

... Human experience of the power of conscious imagining belongs at the same time to the world. That this is so is a consequence of the Mystery of Golgotha. It is the power of Christ that imprints human Imagination into the cosmos; the Christ force that is united with the Earth. So long as this was not united with the Earth but worked onto the Earth from outside as the power of the Sun, all the impulses of life and of growth went into the human interior. Humanity was formed and sustained by them from out of the cosmos. Ever since the Christ impulse has been united with the life of the Earth humans in their self-conscious being are being given back to the cosmos.

Humans have changed from universal into earthly beings. They have the potential to become universal beings again, after they have become *themselves* as earthly beings.[28]

In our age, which is dedicated to a cult of matter and energy, all this may sound very strange, even crazy. However, there are clear signs of a significant turning point in the thinking of leading scientists. The thought that spiritual activity is at the root of everything material and that therefore, if one is consistent, spiritual forces—among which rank our own consciousness—could conceivably be involved in the arising and maintaining of the physical world, loses some of its unlikeliness if one reads, for example, the report given by Herwig Franz Schopper—the general director of the European Centre for Nuclear Research, Cern, near Geneva—when interviewed by the magazine *Der Spiegel* a few years ago. The theme was the successes and hopes of the particle physicists in their search for the basic constituents of nature. Because it is so symptomatic I shall quote verbatim a whole passage out of this thought-provoking conversation:

Spiegel: Would you think that the fact of whether the human being is made of quarks or subquarks could signify a turning point in the realm of philosophy as significant as the one in Copernicus' time?

Schopper: I wouldn't know whether it consists of quarks or subquarks.

But the big question is: are there ultimate, indestructible, impenetrable building stones of matter, as Kant formulated, and which was thought to be so, for instance, by scientific materialism, or does everything dissolve in abstraction?

Spiegel: In energy.

Schopper: Not only that. There are indications that the ultimate principles of nature, the first principles, from which we may some day derive everything, are so-called symmetries. If we were to come to the conclusion that, so to speak, actual reality does not consist of indestructible blocks but abstractions, that would of course have very far-reaching consequences.

We should then discard the idea of Democritus, who was the first to introduce the idea of the atom. We should then move towards Plato, who believed that the ultimate things are ideas, and who said that we see only shadows.

Spiegel: Surely that would be the end of physics!

Schopper: We don't know. We said a number of times over the past 150 years that physics had come to the end. When Max Planck wanted to study physics he was told not to, for physics had reached the end. There are theorists even today who say that in principle everything has been explained.

I think nature is much more inventive than we suppose. There will probably be surprises time and again.[29]

A few examples should be given here to outline the significance of imaginative consciousness. A description is still outstanding of the spiritual rebirth human beings experience when they achieve Imagination, and thereby take a further step towards maturity. So far, when we have spoken of mental images, dreams and so on, we have talked of an 'artistic, picture-creating force'. A real knowing of the human and the natural world—which, as we have shown, can already be had at the level of strengthened thinking—brings one constantly in touch with *beings* and not merely forces. Imaginative consciousness reveals the divine origin behind the widest range of phenomena: every image in nature is a kind of physical coagulation of an Imagination.

Just as the pictures human beings create originate in the soul-spiritual part of them, the natural images around us originate in the soul-spiritual part of the cosmos. In the last resort we are dealing with a cosmic-earthly *force of manifestation*. By means of imaginative consciousness this force acquires clear features, becoming a lofty Being who, in her many different nuances and levels, appears as one who is involved to the greatest extent in the evolution of the human and the natural world. This is the 'Sophia'. In the coming chapters I shall show that she is a Being who concerns us today very much indeed, and whose nature should be grasped as clearly as possible if we really want to understand the foundation and background of life.

The Being and Activity of the Cosmic-earthly Sophia

In contemplating Nature's being,
Know the One as many, seeing
In and outer coinciding,
Nothing in from out dividing
Open secret, revelation!
Grasp it without hesitation.

Free of seeming truth's confusion,
Revel in the serious game!
Separateness is the illusion—
One and many are the same.

Goethe, The 'Epirrhema' (a kind of
epilogue) at the end of his poem
on the metamorphosis of the plant.*

Goethe is pointing to a mysterious relationship between inside and outside in the whole of nature, whereby every phenomenon is the complete expression of something that was previously invisible but which now becomes corporeal: '... On no account look for anything behind the phenomena; they themselves are the message ... Nature conceals God! But not for everybody.'[30]

Novalis clothed this fact in the words: 'Outer nature is inner nature raised to a level of mystery ... We are at one and the same time inside and outside nature.'[31]

Indeed, this polarity of inner–outer, invisible–visible, or being–phenomenon is the primal structural principle of the entire universe. In the various examples of soul imagery we looked at in the first chapter this creative polarity has already been

* Translation by Aldyth Morris, taken from *Goethe's Botanical Writings*, University of Hawaii Press, Honolulu 1952.

evident. Memories, dreams, visions, hallucinations and fantasies are all illustrations, albeit on different levels, whose content is not present in waking consciousness but which manifests in pictures, sounds or some other form similar to sense experience from out of hidden regions of the soul. In this regard Imagination forms no exception in that it also creates 'pictures'. However, the sense-perceptible outer world—its phenomenalism—can likewise be regarded as the manifestation of a hidden element.

Sigismund von Gleich formulates this fact as follows:

> What is phenomenalism then? It is simply *primal being* manifesting itself, the manifestation of *primal substance*. That this substance becomes manifest, visible and knowable is one of its fundamental characteristics: being wants to manifest. *Substance* is the highest of *Aristotle's* categories. We must grasp it today as the duality of *being* and *phenomena*.
>
> ... With the word substance ancient philosophy was referring to primal being, to *God* ... the idea of causality is actually derived from the double category being–phenomenon. Since *John Locke* we have lost our awareness of this. To an ever-increasing extent the pair of concepts being–phenomenon became replaced by cause–effect. And this has been the reason for the almost endless confusion in many areas of natural science, especially in physiology of the senses and the theory of knowledge. What is now called causes and effects are in truth particular instances of being in general or the various forms of manifestation of a particular being. So we should get out of the habit of calling the sense-perceptible cosmos the effect of the 'causes of causes', namely, of God, and formulate the truth by saying that the world is the form of manifestation or the revelation of divine being, the diverse particularization of His universal being.
>
> The concept of causality has led to widespread mechanization of all cosmological concepts. Present-day physics is opening things up again but has not yet put the double category of substance or 'being–phenomenon' in its place. This will not happen until *Goethe's* phenomenalism is recognized as the most

fertile natural scientific method of research and actually put to use.[32]

The concept beauty belongs by nature to the concept manifestation. For, as Goethe once said so pertinently in his prose aphorisms, 'Beauty is a manifestation of secret natural laws which, but for its emergence, would remain forever hidden.'[33]

Here we touch on the whole realm of art where, again, the previous statements apply in full. Let us also bear in mind the well-known principle that Paul Klee expressed in his *Creative Confessions*: 'Art is not a matter of reproducing what is visible but of making things visible.' Indeed, an artist puts what is in his soul into visible and audible form. Art and nature, like the different aspects of consciousness we have discussed, are both subject to the law according to which things of an inner, invisible nature are changed into outer forms. We are dealing fundamentally with a birth process, albeit one that has many levels and is of a universal nature. For what is 'birth' other than the coming into manifestation of something that was previously hidden? Whether it is the birth or conception of a human being or the birth of an Imagination—'. . . be it an idea? or be it life in the becoming?' as Brunetto Latini would say— either way we are dealing with the cosmic-cum-earthly evolutionary law of being–phenomenon. In so far as this applies, this force of manifestation has female character. This is the background for why the spiritual power that 'adorned' the whole cosmos with its visible, sensual qualities and created all the human forms of consciousness appeared to the body-bound, anthropomorphic kind of vision as a female being. We have already referred to the School of Chartres in connection with the symbolic-allegorical thinking principally cultivated there (for example, *Anticlaudianus* by Alanus de Insulis, *c.* 1114–1203, and his description of the Seven Liberal Arts and other beings, all of whom appear as female figures, or Bernardus Silvestris, *fl.* 1153, *De mundi universitate*).[34] Here, too, mighty beings appear in female form, although spiritual beings are beyond sex. These wise scholars of the past did not have the kind of naive picture of natural laws as we, with our dry and sterile intellect, suppose. They saw *different* qualities in humanity and the cosmos than merely those that can be measured and weighed.

Today, the world of phenomena can manifest to our freely conceived Imagination as the 'feminine element' of the cosmos, thus lifting the veil. It is most enlightening that a scientist and artist such as Goethe closes his masterpiece *Faust* with an appearance of 'the eternal feminine'.

Every civilization has had a different name for this Being, referring to very different qualities. In ancient Egypt she was called Isis, in Babylon Ishtar. Hellas recognized both Artemis and Persephone.[35] These are just a couple of examples. In one instance they considered more the aspect of germination and fertility and in the other more the spiritual side.[36] We must bear in mind that the cults around this Being had their rise and their fall—the same as all living things—and we have only to detect where one form comes to an end and where the golden thread re-emerges.

In the realm of Greek Christianity they spoke of the Sophia as the way in which God manifested. Arthur Schult gives a pregnant summary of this Being's activities:

> In many of the old pre-Christian Mysteries they looked on the Universal Mother as the 'Cosmic Virgin' or the 'Cosmic Star Virgin'. As the 'Cosmic Virgin' the Universal Mother gives birth to the whole starry cosmos. As the 'Star Virgin', representing the cosmos of the fixed stars, the Primal Mother gives birth to the Sun. As the 'Sun Virgin' she gives birth to the planets and the Earth. As 'Mother Earth' ... she becomes the mother of earthly humanity.
>
> ... In the Old Testament we encounter the Sophia as the abundance of God's creative ideas, as the divine cosmos of ideas and of the spirit. In the proverbs of Solomon the Sophia says of herself:

> The Lord possessed me in the beginning of his way, before His
> works of old.
> I was set up from everlasting, from the beginning, or ever the
> Earth was ...
> When He prepared the heavens I was there ... When He
> appointed the foundations of the Earth:
> Then I was by him, as one brought up with him ...
>> (Proverbs 8:22–30)

In the Wisdom of Solomon it says of the Sophia:

> For she is the brightness of the everlasting light, the unspotted
> mirror of the power of God, and the image of His goodness.
> And being but one, she can do all things, and remaining in
> herself, she maketh all things new: and in all ages entering into
> holy souls, she maketh them friends of God and prophets.
>> (Wisdom of Solomon 7:26–27)

> ... She is the wisdom of God, then she is cosmic wisdom and
> finally human wisdom. She inspires all peoples, religions and
> Mysteries. However, in the course of history she overshadows
> particularly that nation which was to prepare the body for the
> Christ-Logos. Sophia worked more and more strongly into the
> spiritual and earthly Zion until, in Mary and the Christ, the
> Mystery of the birth of the Son of Man became full earthly
> reality.[37]

Here, too, there is a reference to the two poles of her being:
the Universal Mother of the Earth and mankind and the
mother of all the wisdom in the cosmos and in human beings.
The Mystery of the Christ-Mary is also mentioned. Before we
look, in the next chapter, at the *merging of these three aspects*
and their intensification in the events at the turning point of
time, let us sketch the path of the Christ and the Sophia to
human beings.

As also the Christ Logos, this lofty Being is moving towards
humanity from out of regions of cosmic spiritland. A
significant stage of revelation of this Being was in the Isis of
the ancient Egyptian Hermes initiation. The Mysteries of Isis,

which must not be confused with the much later Isis cults of Roman times, revealed, right into the time of Moses, deep insights into the birth processes of the cosmic soul.

Not until the neophyte had worked for many years at the purification of his being and had successfully undergone the trials did he participate in initiation, whereby he was reborn as a messenger of the Gods in order to put his newly acquired forces and capacities at the service of cultural progress. Imagine a dark and solemn place of worship with a kind of grave in the middle. The novice, clad in white, surrounded by the chanting priests, fell into a deathlike sleep lasting about three and a half days. During this time his soul with its core of ego-being left the physical body, which remained behind in the coldness of the sarcophagus. His vision soared up to the spiritual dimensions of the Earth and the cosmos hidden from day consciousness. The person being initiated had all manner of experiences as his vision continued to expand. He felt divine Beings in the form of Sun forces building up his bodily being, and this gave him a deeper knowledge of the etheric processes working in his body, a knowledge which he might well apply later on as a doctor-priest. Yet nothing answered the question he had been struggling with for many years: that of his true origin, the origin of his spiritual soul. At a certain point in his experiences he felt as though he were being received by a great Being from whom shone forth light and warmth.[38]

> And the first impression one gets of this Being is that in this Being reside the forces that carry the soul from one incarnation to the other, reside also the forces that illumine the soul between death and a new birth ... You are feeling the force and the light that emanate from this Being. And you feel bound to ask this Being: Who art thou? for you alone can tell me what you are, and only then shall I know what bears me in my innermost being from death into a new birth. Only if you tell me can I know what is my innermost human core! And the Being to whom one feels so connected remains silent. One feels one is connected with this Being in the deepest part of oneself.

However she remains dumb, and a tremendous longing fills one's soul to solve this universal riddle. One's whole longing flows into this Being, and after a while

> this Being ... gives birth to something that comes forth from her like another Being. But what is born is not like an earthly birth. One knows at once through one's vision that it is not like an earthly birth. No, an earthly birth comes about in time. One sees in one's vision that what is being born has been in the process of being born since primeval times—for eternity—and this birth stretches from primeval times right into the present ... one tells oneself: 'A Being has constantly been in the process of being born by this Being you have united yourself with; but now the process of birth and the Being who is born have become visible to you.'

This is Isis, from whom the human soul receives warmth and light in its innermost being; and the Being who is coming to birth in an ocean of light and music of the spheres, and with whom the human ego feels united in its deepest being, is Osiris, a revelation of the creative cosmic Word, the Christ-Logos. The deepest self-knowledge of one's own humanity rooted in the spiritual ground of the cosmos became for the neophyte an impression never to be extinguished. And when the hierophant then called the initiated one back into earthly existence he could speak about being newly born in Isis and Osiris. In mythological tradition Osiris is spoken of as the husband and the son of Isis.

One approaches the deeper meaning of this riddle if one sees the being of Isis as sheath of the purest selflessness—another word for love—who offers herself to that which comes from a higher sphere and as it were 'fructifies' her in order to manifest *through* her. That which is born—the 'son'—was already there, and she brings him to manifestation. At the first stage Osiris is her husband and at the second stage her son, and she holds the creative centre as the essence of love, receiving and giving birth. The newborn Osiris is also called Horus.

In later times this experience could no longer be attained, for the Sun Logos Himself was preparing to be born in Palestine in a human body, which happened at the Baptism in the Jordan. Isis became the mourning widow.

The important dividing line was at the time of Moses, for Moses, who had been initiated into the Egyptian Mysteries, by

> leading his people out of Egypt, took with him ... the part of the Egyptian initiation that added the Osiris initiation to the mourning Isis, as she became later on. This is how the transition from Egyptian culture to the culture of the Old Testament came about. Indeed, Moses had taken with him the Mystery of Osiris, the Mystery of the Cosmic Word! And if he had not left behind him the powerless Isis there would not have sounded forth for him what he had to hear in the form necessary for his people: the significant words 'I am the I-am, ejeh asher ejeh'.[39] In this way the Egyptian Mysteries were led over to the ancient Hebrew Mysteries.

The initiates in the Mysteries could no longer find Osiris and they were called from then onwards 'sons of the widow'.[40] The Sun Logos, who had revealed himself through the form of Osiris, would now reveal himself as the bearer of the forces of the I-am from out of the elemental sheath of the Earth, in fire and cloud and in the lightning on Sinai. From the spiritual-soul heights of the cosmos he had reached the elemental sheath of the Earth—the Persephone aspect, the nature aspect of the Sophia-Isis—as his new plane of manifestation until, at the turning point of time, she became *the most devoted bearer of the whole force of the Christ in the present and into the future.*

The Sophia path of wisdom also reached an important stage of its development in Palestine. As the carrying principle of any and every manifestation of consciousness she united herself especially with the very capacity that had to take over from atavistic vision, in order to inaugurate a form of knowledge based on the ego, namely, the capacity of thinking.

Rudolf Steiner places Abraham at the beginning of this

process. He lived *c*. 2100 BC. In Abraham and his descendants the divine Sophia took up her connection with thinking in that she revealed herself in those people for the first time in the physical body:

> Abraham was the first to develop the inward reflection of divine wisdom, of divine perception in a truly human way, as human thoughts concerning the Godhead ... Abraham was, in fact, the first to develop the physical instrument of thinking. Therefore he is not wrongly ... called the inventor of arithmetic, as arithmetic is pre-eminently a science of thought dependent on the physical body as an instrument ... To contemplate the Godhead in thought requires a physical instrument, and this organ was implanted for the first time in Abraham.[41]

In the course of history this capacity became the common property of mankind. In a rhythm of about seven hundred years the Sophia, in her ability to manifest thinking, united more and more deeply with human consciousness.[42] The whole evolution of philosophy mirrors her path. From about the year 1400 AD she united with the beginnings of the consciousness soul, to bring about, from our time on, Imagination. Events of the greatest importance, however, were to take place at the turning point of time, so we shall now look at this moment in time.

The Mystery of Isis-Sophia
at the Turning Point of Time

The riddles connected with why the exalted Sophia Being works in such different ways among the various peoples can be solved if we bear in mind that her appearances as a Being have come about within the framework of a series of hierarchical stages. Hierarchies of this kind engaging in the developmental processes of our cosmos are a substantial part of every spiritual tradition and spiritual practice of any significance right into our century, as Rudolf Steiner's anthroposophy testifies.

The workings of these Beings who, as in the case of the Hierarchies of Angels, are also anchored in Christian tradition, are connected with a certain primal phenomenon, with a law that can be called the law of spiritual transparency.

The more perfect a spiritual being is—the more open or transparent it is to a still higher order—the more perfect it can become in its own qualities, just as a coloured glass window does not look its best until the sun shines through it (the word transparent comes from the Latin *transparere* and means as good as shining through). In a similar way Angel Beings can be filled with higher Beings in a gesture of spiritual openness to the realm above. And the fullness of the Godhead can be present in ever more widespread realms. We can also imagine the complex workings of the great Isis-Sophia taking place in this way and, as indicated in the previous chapter, coming nearer and nearer to the human world. As the maternal sheath of the Christ she united herself with the whole of humanity and the Earth in order to join with her 'Son' in the building of a new creation: the heavenly Jerusalem, as John describes in the twenty-first chapter of his Apocalypse.

We find her again at decisive stages of the Christ revelation. By way of example let us pick three outstanding passages from

the Gospels: the Baptism in the Jordan, the Event of
Golgotha, and Whitsun, the festival of the outpouring of the
Holy Spirit.

The Baptism in the Jordan, recorded in all four Gospels,
presents the tremendous event of the birth of Christ, the Son
of God, in the man Jesus. Let us quote the testimonies of Luke
and of John:

> Now it happened
> When all the people had been baptized
> And Jesus had not been baptized
> And was praying
> That the heaven was opened
> And the Holy Spirit
> Descended on Him
> In visible form
> As a dove
>
> And a voice came out of heaven
> You are my Son
> The beloved
> Today I have brought you to birth.[43]
>
> Now they had been sent out
> By the pharisees
> And they asked him
> Why are you baptizing
> if you are neither the Christ
> Nor Elijah
> Nor the Prophet?
> John answered them
> I myself baptize in water
> He stands among you
> Whom indeed you do not know
> He is the one
> Who comes after me
> And I
> I am not worthy
> To undo the strap of his sandal

All this took place in Bethany
Beyond the Jordan
Where John was baptizing
The next day
He saw Jesus coming towards him
And said
Look on the Lamb of God
The bearer of the sin of the world
This is he
Of whom I myself said
One grown to manhood comes after me
Who existed before me
Because he preceded me
I indeed did not know him
In order that he should be shown to
Israel
I
I have come
Baptizing in water
And John bore witness
Thus I beheld the Spirit
Descending as a dove from heaven
And remaining on him
I indeed did not know him
But the one who sent me
To baptize in water
Is the one who said to me
He on whom you see the Spirit descending
And remaining on him
He it is
Who will baptize in Holy Spirit
And I
I have perceived
And have borne witness
That this is the Son of God.[44]

This dove 'remaining on him' is a clairvoyantly-perceived image of the presence of the Holy Spirit in this tremendous inner birth process.

Jesus filled himself with the power of the Holy Spirit, which brought about in him the birth of the Christ, the creative Logos. This higher birth was enabled to happen by the pure transparency of His soul, and here again we recognize the activity of the Sophia. Indeed, this has to do with another, deeper manifestation of the polarity we have already mentioned, namely, being–phenomenon. This gives us a momentary insight into the deepest Christian Mystery that was to move Christendom for centuries: the Mystery of the Trinity— of the Father, the Son and the Holy Spirit. Out of unrevealed worlds of the spirit, out of the 'Father', through the birth-giving force of the Holy Sophia-Spirit, the Christ Logos is born *in* Jesus of Nazareth. The Son of God will come to manifestation *through* Jesus, and the Son reveals himself more and more as the force that is capable of bestowing the strongest impulses on the whole evolution of the Earth and mankind: 'And lo, I am with you always, even unto the end of Earth days.'[45] The man Jesus had sacrificed his own individuality. Seen from the aspect of the creation, the Christ Logos is the force that works in between those of invisible being and visible phenomenon, as the creative transition between them as it were. The Christ Logos possesses creative impulses drawn from the inner nature of the Father, the divine All, which are the inspiration for the primal plan of the force of revelation of the Sophia-Holy Spirit. This 'plan'or *meaning* inherent in a cosmic language, the letters, syllables and words of which are in visible nature, needs the pure, selfless forces of the Sophia to enable it to manifest. She, the Holy Spirit, who has been symbolized throughout the centuries as a dove coming from on high, supplies the loving sheath essential to any true birth. In many religions we encounter the dove as a sacred creature, and in the Song of Solomon it is like an appearance of the Goddess Natura, who speaks out of ravines in the rocks and who is 'lovely' to behold. Her white plumage is an imaginative picture for the purity of this Being whose home is in cosmic heights and who possesses selfless sacrificial forces. Was not the dove the creature of sacrifice in the various cults of pre-Christian times?[46] The trinity working as a unity: invisible, divine Being—creative impulse—visible creation, or, Father, Son and Holy Spirit, became, with Christ Jesus, with whom the dove remained united, a fully historical event of Earth evolution. Henceforth He will reveal the Father in the aspect of a new creation of the Earth and of humanity, as the New Testament tells us so impressively.

This is the central aspect of this scene at the Jordan which is so powerful and yet unobtrusive and which, as archetypal phenomenon, is open to new levels of interpretation.

We now want to look at one of these interpretations with reference to the previous chapter, namely, that it can be looked at as an earthly realization of the birth Mystery of Isis who now indeed gives birth to the sunlike son who is the essence of the deepest ego forces, that God who answered Moses in the burning bush with the words: 'I am the I-am.' This birth took place in Jesus of Nazareth and became an archetype for all future initiations in the Christian Mysteries. Just as the Egyptian neophyte experienced his actual initiation in the process of identification with the birth of the Sun Word, the true Christian initiate must in future say in the words of Paul: 'But when it pleased God, who ... called me by His grace, to reveal his son in me', and further: 'Yet not I, but Christ liveth in me.'[47] This means, however, that each individual person can experience his own baptism in the Jordan in this very sense of spiritual transparency we mentioned at the beginning, which occurs as the result of an intimate inner transformation. The 'old' human being must die, as Jesus did, so that a new human being can be born. It is at the moment of Damascus, in the experience of the light of the resurrected Christ, that we see the central turning point in Paul's own inner transformation. The 'outer' Christ light became the innermost light of consciousness in his own ego, which became capable of infinite growth. Paul did not experience 'possession' from then on for, on the contrary, he grasped hold of his

most individual ego forces which resided in the Christ Logos
as the source of all egohood.

Christ's incarnation into Earth conditions reached its
deepest point in the descent into the depths of the Earth
through the death on Golgotha. The 'descent into hell', as
later centuries called Christ's descent into the depths of death
and evil, can also be seen as a part of a cosmic birth process.

The Gospels are silent on this point, but if we look at the
middle cross standing out in such stark relief from the dark
background it is as though the dove were presenting itself
again as the image of the beginning of a new birth that is made
real through the deepest sense of sacrifice. At Easter there
comes forth from Mother Earth, into which the corpse was
lowered, a body of light—that light that will shine with such
power at the hour of Damascus. And the consequences of this
event, as described by Paul, in his letter to the Romans, and
John, in the penultimate chapter of the Apocalypse, will be
that human beings *and* the Earth will participate in a transformation. The Earth will become the new Jerusalem, the
'bride of the lamb', expressions used by the writer of the
Apocalypse to indicate the 'feminine' nature of this new form
of the Earth. The 'lamb' is here an image of the pure power of
sacrifice of the Christ Logos, which attained its climax on
Golgotha.

As early as Whitsun the Risen One was to become inti-
mately connected with the inner being of each individual in the
image of the bright flames, to seal the new birth 'with the Holy
Spirit and with fire'. This scene, taking place in the midst of
'the rushing of a mighty wind',[48] shows the people present
there to be the bearers of a new language, a new wisdom that
can be understood by everyone.

As long ago as the Indian Vedas we find Agni, the Fire God
of sacrifice. Heraclitus, the sage of Ephesus, spoke of the
creative primal fire, the Logos, thus indicating the dynamic
depths of the Godhead. Flame is meant here as the imaginative expression of the inner nature of Christ, in the sense of a

process of dying and becoming. Fire arises when a substance is burnt, as it were sacrificing itself, and when 'wind' or relatively speaking pure air constantly rekindles it. This is a wonderful picture for a steady growth through change, which means in other words a perpetually renewing rebirth, for human beings have a long way to go.

A spiritual birth and *simultaneously* a new manifestation of wisdom: in the miracle of Whitsun, an anticipation of the stages of human development, all the aspects of birth and of wisdom of Isis-Sophia, were intensified. And from then on the figure of Mary, who had conceived the child under the 'overshadowing of the Holy Spirit',[49] was felt and understood to be the image of the Mystery, just as Angelus Silesius has put into words in his *Cherubinischer Wandersmann*, among other instances:

> If your soul is virgin and pure as Mary's was,
> God will presently make it fertile.

> If Christ is born a thousand times in Bethlehem
> And not in you, you will be lost eternally.

In a special way the activity of Sophia became increasingly visible *through* Mary.[50] Many painters have, with justification, placed her in the centre of the Whitsun event; for they knew that if Mary is in the centre the spiritual flame nature of the human being can be reborn.

Emil Bock, a profound connoisseur of the being of Mary, writes that the image of Mary can be especially informative for the people of our own time

> concerning both the most distant past and the furthest future of mankind's evolution. Humanity stands as it were between two polar opposite forms of salvation. In the past we were intimately connected with the divine world. We have forfeited this connection and lost Paradise. However, in the figure of Mary we have a bodily memory of our original closeness to God and the spirit. And at one and the same time this figure contains the

potential of something that humanity cannot fully bring to realization until the end of earthly time. Let us try therefore ... to look at the figures at the crib in Bethlehem not only as historical memories but also as figures in which we perhaps recognize ourselves—in what we *no longer* are or have *not yet* become.

These figures round the crib are unique; they cannot come again in that way in the whole course of human history. These figures have so to speak descended from Heaven onto the Earth and become human. This conception is familiar to us with regard to the Christ Himself. We are familiar with the thought that a Being who once belonged to the highest regions of divinity became man. He chose to incarnate on Earth. Already in pre-Christian times there was this God who dies and rises again. Whether he was called Osiris in the Egyptian era or Adonis in Phoenician times, people knew of the risen God and celebrated him in the cults of the seasons together with nature. This God, who dies and rises again, now descends from Heaven and becomes man.

However, before this occurred another Being descended from Heaven to Earth. At all events this Being, whom the ancient Egyptians, for instance, regarded as the Goddess Isis with the child Horus, and whom nations all over the world right into the Far East knew as the Virgin Mother Goddess, was mirrored in the human figure of Mary. At the turning point of time we see this image of the Virgin Mother with her child in her arms in the most simple human form: the girlish mother from Nazareth who gave birth to a child in a rocky cave in Bethlehem, far from her native place. Here we encounter two fundamental Mysteries of humanity: the child in the crib will grow up; he will be seen by the world suffering the lot of being human, and will overcome through the resurrection what was previously known in the Mystery temples of all peoples as the Mystery of death. And in the figure of Mary we encounter the Mysteries of birth. The Goddess who gives birth and yet remains virgin: this is the other pole of the Mystery of humanity.

... So another necessity for today is to rediscover a Mystery that already existed in the first Christian centuries. Knowledge of it was in fact the reason why in the first Christian millennium people actually did not speak of Mary but maintained a tactful silence. Mary was not even portrayed in pictures. In the West there are virtually no pictures of Mary before the year 1000 AD. It was not until late medieval times, when the Church saw the advantage of proclaiming the Mary cult, that there arose pictures into which flowed so much feeling and presentiment ... Only to think of the Madonnas of Raphael! Yet in the early days the Madonna was portrayed very seldom, just because people knew there was a Mystery there that appeared to be greater than could be portrayed in picture-form. This most holy of Mysteries, too great even to be spoken of, was a knowledge of the connection between Mary and the Holy Spirit; Mary was felt to be an incarnation of the Holy Spirit. In certain areas of Bavaria and Austria one often still finds medieval pictures of the Christian Trinity in which are portrayed the Father God, Christ and then Mary in the place of the Holy Spirit.[51]

Among the most moving things that Rudolf Steiner communicated to us from his spiritual research is the fact that at the moment of the Baptism in the Jordan Mary was actually filled with the being of the Sophia—the Holy Spirit—and that they subsequently remained united.[52]

The new, combined activity of the Sophia-Christ Being, as occurring in archetypal form in the Whitsun miracle, should benefit humanity more and more. Human beings have been privileged to be bearers of this healing stream, and especially in the circles around the Holy Grail. In the knights who wore the emblem of the dove, we see an important stage of this activity.

Michelangelo's *Pietà* and the Grail

There is a motif that appears in the fine arts around 1300 and then again and again in the succeeding centuries, the motif of the *pietà*. The presentation of Mary holding the dead Jesus in her lap reached an artistic climax in the well-known *Pietà* that a French cardinal commissioned the 24-year-old Michelangelo to carry out, and which can be seen today in the Church of St Peter in Rome (see illustration on page 48).

This sculpture has a special atmosphere. One is struck by the chaste girlishness of Mary, which makes her look younger than her son, and the open gesture with which she seems to be reflecting on his death: as though she had taken this death into herself, right into a sphere of purity and calm, of silence in fact, where a Mystery appears to be being enacted. The body of Jesus is dead and given over entirely to Earth heaviness—and yet his veins are pulsing with blood. Christ, who lived and died as a human being, is the size of an average person, whereas Mary is larger than lifesize. Did Michelangelo wish to portray by this that the Virgin Mother is filled with a higher element? This *Pietà* is at any rate a work of deep Christian piety, and anyone looking at it with an open mind will receive a lasting impression.

It seems to us as though an important aspect of the Sophia-Christ mystery is captured in this sculpture in a form which was the only way an artist of the Renaissance—committed as he was to the earthly world of form—could express it. Mary's garment, in which the dead body appears to be enveloped, is large and protective, and so alive in the sweeping lines of the innumerable folds that it gives the impression of a maternal womb in which new life is beginning to stir. The whole sculpture speaks a language of gesture that is so gentle and chaste that it is in no way obtrusive and leaves the observer

Pietà by Michelangelo, Church of St Peter, Rome

totally free. It is worthy of note that a similar *pietà* motif appeared about three hundred years previously, in poetry, describing significant stages of the path of initiation of a 'son of the widow'—Mysteries to do with world and self-knowledge. Michelangelo created this sculpture in 1498/1499, and Wolfram von Eschenbach completed his *Parzival c.* 1210.

A path to the Grail, to the highest goals of earthly aspirations as conceived in those times, is depicted in *Parzival* in wonderful imagery, in genuine literary Imaginations. In this path to the Grail we recognize the fundamental character of the ancient Isis initiation, now in a Christianized form and transformed into earthly paths of destiny. Only when we realize the significance of the 'feminine' Sophia element in the whole ritual can the curtain be raised upon the sacred part of the Grail and show us vast perspectives of the Christ-Sophia stream in history. Among the great Grail poets of the Middle Ages it is Wolfram von Eschenbach in particular who gives this motif such a significant form.

Let us look from this point of view at a few striking passages from *Parzival*.

Herzeloyde, now a widow, retires into the forest of Soltane to protect her son from any contact with knights. He must not encounter the same fate as his father. Parzival grows up remote from all worldly activity until one day he meets, in the forest, some knights from the court of King Arthur. The sight of these dazzling figures in shining armour astride their gallant steeds is at the same time a premonition of his inner calling, as though he saw in them an image of a more noble humanity which has firm control over its animal nature, taming it for the attainment of high goals. The young Parzival is seized by a great yearning to become such a knight. He wants to go to Arthur and he deserts his mother, not knowing that she thereupon dies of a broken heart. He is entirely ignorant of the fact that he is behaving on every occasion like a fool and— following solely the law of his own egoism—is time and again bringing distress upon other people. He grew up without knowledge of the world or of other people, and it was to be a long time before he awoke to his true destiny, until he learnt that the greatest wisdom springs from questions arising out of true compassion. He sets forth into the world to find himself and will release a fellow sufferer, thereby becoming the Grail King.

When he left his mother he did not even know what his name was. Not until he meets Sigune, the grieving maiden with her dead bridegroom in her lap, is he told his true name, which means in the language of Wolfram that he is led to an important stage of self-knowledge, for this encounter is to stamp itself profoundly on his subconscious:

> Thus our simple boy came riding down a slope. He heard a woman's voice. There, beside a cliff, a lady was wailing in real anguish. Her true joy had been torn in twain. The lad quickly rode over to her. Now hear what the lady was doing. There was Sigune tearing her long brown braids out of her head for grief. The lad looked, and there was Shianatulander the Prince, dead in the maiden's lap. She was aweary of all mirth ...
>
> She said to the lad: 'You have virtue in you. Honour be to your sweet youth and to your lovely face! In truth you will be rich in blessings. This knight did not die by the javelot, he perished in a joust. Fidelity was born in you, that you can feel pity this way for him.' Before she allowed the lad to ride on she asked him his name, remarking that he showed the evidence of God's handiwork.
>
> 'Bon fils, cher fils, beau fils, that is what I was called by those who knew me at home.'
>
> As soon as he said this she recognized him by those names. Now hear him more correctly named so that you will know who is the lord of this adventure.
>
> As he stood there with the maiden her red mouth made haste to speak: 'In truth your name is Parzival, which signifies "Right through the middle". Such a furrow did great love plough in your mother's heart with the plough of her faithfulness. Your father bequeathed her sorrow. I tell you, and not to boast, your mother is my aunt ...'[53]

We can feel this to be the motif of the grieving Isis who guards a person's real secret, his 'name', but in this case it is now interwoven in Parzival's life as a fateful encounter. He is actually indirectly involved in this death, for Shianatulander died defending Parzival's inheritence from Duke Orilus. He will encounter these again, three more times, at important crisis points in his destiny. An observant reader will realize that the whole plot hinges on this *pietà* motif.

Although *Parzival* was written out of a historical background[54] the epic describes primarily the inner path of him who is destined to be the Grail King. Wolfram is speaking to people who still have a feeling that real images are at the same time symbols for soul-spiritual realities. Everybody can rediscover themselves at some point of this poem, for, however individual Parzival's path was from one point of view, from another point of view it is just as much an archetypal picture of a humanity which, since the Mystery of Golgotha, no longer has to undergo initiation in the closed precincts of a temple but in the confrontations with everyday life. Each event is a picture of an inner maturing on the path to the Grail.

How does Wolfram von Eschenbach regard the 'Grail' about which so much was being written in his time?

Parzival leaves Sigune and on the search for his mother comes by way of various experiences and adventures, as though by accident, into the region of the Grail. A short while before he had freed the besieged town of Pelrapeire and married its Queen Conduiramour. Coming through a cleft in the rock he finds the path to the Grail and is ceremoniously welcomed. The King, Amfortas, has succumbed to an illness he has brought upon himself and is suffering immensely. The intensity of his egoistic impulses, which we see depicted in the image of a bleeding spear that is carried past at the beginning of the Grail scene, has plunged him into the deepest misery. Only someone capable of asking the right question can redeem him. But Parzival will fail.

We see him sitting with the King and many other knights in

a magnificent hall, when suddenly a steel door opens and 24 maidens in costly attire enter. Wolfram cannot find words enough to describe their splendour. Then there appears Repanse de Schoye, the maiden who carries the Grail:

> After them came the Queen. So radiant was her countenance that everyone thought the dawn was breaking. She was clothed in a dress of Arabian silk. Upon a deep green achmardi she bore the perfection of Paradise, both root and branch. That was a thing called the Grail, which surpasses all earthly perfection. Repanse de Schoye was the name of her whom the Grail permitted to be its bearer. Such was the nature of the Grail that she who watched over it had to preserve her purity and renounce all falsity.
>
> Before the Grail came lights of no small worth, six vessels of clear glass, tall and beautifully formed, in which balsam was burning sweetly. When they had advanced a proper distance from the door the Queen and all the maidens bearing the balsam bowed courteously. Then the Queen free of falsity placed the Grail before the host.[55]

The Grail provided a miracle of feasting, but food not only of an earthly kind for it immediately says: 'For the Grail was the fruit of blessedness, such abundance of the sweetness of the world that its delights were very like what we are told of the Kingdom of Heaven.'[56]

What gives the Grail such power? We discover this in the ninth book, in which the hermit Trevrizent gives the straying Parzival a significant piece of advice regarding the Grail. We discover at the same time that the Grail knights, who do good deeds throughout the world, draw their strength from the Grail. Important images now appear which, like the *pietà* motif, remind us of the events in Palestine; they are like a veil for that which is concealed behind Repanse de Schoye and the Grail.

> '... Well I know,' said his host, 'that many brave knights dwell with the Grail at Monsalvaesche. Always when they ride out, as

they often do, it is to seek adventure. They do so for their sins, these Templars, whether their reward be defeat or victory. A valiant host lives there, and I will tell you how they are sustained. They live from a stone of purest kind. If you do not know it, it shall here be named to you. It is called "lapsit exillis". By the power of that stone the phoenix burns to ashes, but the ashes give him life again. Thus does the phoenix moult and change its plumage, which afterwards is bright and shining and as lovely as before. There never was a human so ill but that if he one day sees that stone he cannot die within the week that follows. And in looks he will not fade. His appearance will stay the same, be it maid or man, as on the day he saw the stone ... Such power does the stone give a man that flesh and bones are at once made young again. The stone is also called the Grail.

'This very day there comes to it a message wherein lies its greatest power. Today is Good Friday, and they await there a dove, winging down from Heaven. It brings a small white wafer, and leaves it on the stone. Then, shining white, the dove soars up to Heaven again. Always on Good Friday it brings to the stone what I have just told you, and from that the stone derives whatever good fragrances of drink and food there are on Earth, like to the perfection of Paradise...'[57]

It is not difficult to see in the dove who lays the wafer (an expression of the life forces) on the stone, a kind of picture in miniature of the Baptism in the Jordan—the stone being the picture for the forces of the physical-mineral body into which a rejuvenating force enters, is 'born' out of divine cosmic heights; a process that reached its climax on the very first Good Friday. What Trevrizent is describing here are experiences of a spiritual vision he reached in his contemplation. He knows the nature of the forces which come from the Christ-Sophia Being, as we would say in this context, and which work right into the body in a transfiguring, rejuvenating way. And this applies in principle for everybody even today, only that each person must find their own way to it, as Trevrizent did, and eventually Parzival also does, after the question born out of his heart makes him King of the Grail and bearer of the forces of resurrection, as we see with such clarity in the redemption scene:

> All in tears then, Parzival said, 'Tell me where the Grail is kept here. If God's goodness triumphs in me, this throng of people shall be witness to it.'
>
> Then, facing in that direction, he genuflected thrice in honour of the Trinity, praying that help might be vouchsafed for this sorrowful man's pain of heart. He rose to his feet again and said, 'Uncle, what is it that troubles you?'
>
> He who for St Sylvester's sake brought a bullock back to life from the dead, and who bade Lazarus arise, the same gave help that Amfortas was healed and made well again. The lustre which the French call 'fleur' came over his flesh.[58]

We see that the whole epic is ultimately a song of praise to Isis-Sophia as the sheath of the Risen One with His power to be a saviour and to overcome death. To summarize briefly: a shining dove renews each Good Friday the miraculous power of the stone. When the *Whitsun community* of knights is gathered—turtle doves are depicted on their coat-of-arms—the Grail can be brought in. Repanse de Schoye, accompanied by 24 maidens, who all have particular duties to perform, steps through the door into the hall and the feast can begin. All these are images of the 'eternal feminine'.

And Sigune?

Let us return to the *pietà* motif, for it complements the Grail images in a significant way. The *pietà* is basically an image which, since the Mystery of Golgotha, lives deep in every human soul. At its deepest level it is identical with the Christ-Sophia. To be aware of this is at the same time a new birth, for at this level consciousness is a creative force. It produces in the human being a new person as the bearer of new powers of wisdom, as we saw in Trevrizent, through the might of selfless love.

Human beings, whether women or men, who experience this rebirth in the sign of the Holy Spirit, become in spirit part of the original Whitsun community. Wherever they are active, whether as simple people or as scholars, they bear within themselves, as an inexhaustible force for their daily work the phoenix fire they have by virtue of their belonging to Christ-Sophia. The paths to the Grail were inner ones. Nevertheless, the work of the true 'Grail knights' was entirely in and for the world. As it was then, so it is today and so it will be in the future. Wolfram von Eschenbach, among others, knew this.

Parzival travelled these paths, which did not avoid error and guilt, as a striking example of the kind of human being who is learning anew to ask questions. An individual's questions will replace the domination of secular and ecclesiastical institutions and be a pledge of inner freedom. As we learn from *Parzival*, questions are already the start of a new birth of the entire person. Searching for an answer involves error, error involves guilt, as we witness in the future king's struggles to come to the Grail. Along this path his encounters with Sigune became the many layers of a veil he had to lift to reach his true goal. After Amfortas has been redeemed, which is at the same time Parzival's redemption, her mission has been fulfilled.

She is an image of the primal force of the soul itself, grieving for a part of the human being killed by the egoism of selfish desires. To be aware of her means to develop feelings of guilt with regard to every injustice occurring in the world, for one feels co-responsible, as Parzival does later on, in the most painful self-knowledge. Only in the course of purifying his soul forces does the striving human being pass through his own *pietà* image to the birth of the 'Christ in me'.

We can understand from all these things that Rudolf Steiner could say the following:

> . . . there appeared again something the submergence of which had been witnessed by those souls weighed down by a tragic mood, namely, the ones who were undergoing initiation in the late Egyptian Mysteries. When it appeared it could be seen by the ones who were privileged to participate in the Mysteries in

later times. And what they could thus see reappearing—
reappearing, however, in a way that now belonged to Earth
evolution—they had to form into a picture.

And what was this form taken by that which had disappeared in ancient Egypt?

It reappeared by becoming visible in the holy vessel, which is
called the 'Holy Grail', which is guarded by the knights of the
Holy Grail. In the arising of the Holy Grail we can sense that
which disappeared in ancient Egypt. With the appearance of
the Holy Grail there stands before us the whole Christian
renewal of the ancient Mysteries.[59]

Rudolf Steiner said this in February 1913. About a year
later he describes in lectures dedicated to the theme of the
Grail how the picture of the *Pietà* became so important for his
own spiritual research. He describes among other things how
when he was once coming out of St Peter's Church in Rome

under the strong impression made on me by Michelangelo's
work, which you find on the right hand side as you enter—the
mother with Jesus, the mother who looks so young, with Jesus,
already dead, on her knees. And under the after-effect of
looking at this work of art there came to me, not as a vision but
as a true Imagination from the spiritual world, the picture
showing how Parzival, after he has gone away for the first time
from the castle of the Grail, where he had failed to ask about
the Mysteries which prevail there, meets in the forest a young
woman who is holding her bridegroom in her lap and weeping
over him. But I knew that whether it is the mother or the bride
whose bridegroom is dead (Christ is often called the bridegroom) the picture had a meaning.[60]

On a later occasion, when using another name for Isis, he
says the following about this meaning:

Let us stand in front of the Virgin Mother with the Christ upon
her knees, and let us then express it thus: whoever can feel the
holiness of this image will feel the same for the Holy Grail.
Above all other lights, all other gods, shines the holy vessel—

the Moon Mother now touched by Christ, the new Eve, the
bearer of the Sun-Spirit, Christ.[61]

Isis-Sophia in our Time and the Battle for Imagination

To summarize briefly what has been brought so far, starting from the kind of consciousness present-day human beings have, we set out to find a level of knowledge that really forms a balance between the flood of general information on the one hand and narrow specialization on the other. We referred to the importance of a deepening of consciousness appropriate to the times arising out of independent, ego-active thinking as distinct from the merely receptive soul condition of earlier centuries. We clearly saw a beginning in this direction in the work of Goethe. The first upward step in human consciousness, this Imagination, also called 'heart thinking'[62] by Rudolf Steiner, was described in relation to the individual, to society and to the creation of a new cosmos. It then transpired that Imagination is the 'fruit' of qualitatively distinct image-creating forces in us human beings. Our human consciousness in all its manifestations was also examined from the point of view of being–manifestation, and we drew attention to the fact that the whole visible cosmos in and around us is likewise embedded in this dynamic-creative polarity. *One* revelationary impulse works at *different* levels of inner and outer being according to the spirit of the times.

The kind of thinking that accords with reality encounters not only forces but also spiritual Beings. We spoke of the Being Isis-Sophia as the 'Mother' of all births, physical and spiritual. Like the Sun-Logos Christ she accompanied humanity along its path of development until the moment came when she took part in the events at the turning point of time in a form which entailed tremendous concentration of her activity. Prior to that she had been the focal point of the Egyptian Hermes initiation, but also the bearer of cosmic-earthly wisdom or the power of intelligence altogether. In the Holy Spirit of the Christian Trinity she reveals as it were her highest origin. Many of the world's peoples, especially the leading civilizations, know of her activity even though it appears in very different nuances.

In the Whitsun event both poles of her being, birth on the nature level and birth on the consciousness level, were united and intensified in that the birth of a new wisdom was at the same time the new birth of the flaming ego being of everyone present there. The nucleus of a future Earth, which had its beginnings in the Resurrection Mystery of Sophia-Christ, began to gleam forth. The Grail stream was not only a revival of the Egyptian Mystery culture, for the redeeming power of Golgotha was also active in it as an ongoing force.

The world of the Grail Imaginations disappeared in the centuries when humanity became alienated from the spirit, and the lowest point of this alienation was destined to be in our epoch, the age of the consciousness soul. The true community of the Rosicrucians carried forward the torch of esoteric Christianity[63] until a new impulse, suited to our different state of human consciousness, became necessary. The path of knowledge of anthroposophy then took over, based as it is on a new culture of questioning: 'Anthroposophy is a way of knowledge that can lead the human spirit to the spirit in the universe. It appears in us as a need of the heart and the feelings. It is justified to the extent that it satisfies these needs. Anthroposophy will be recognized solely by those people who find in it what they are looking for in their deepest hearts.' Rudolf Steiner goes on to say that only those people can accept anthroposophy 'who harbour certain questions about the nature of the human being and the world with the same intensity as they feel hunger and thirst.'[64]

To avoid misunderstandings let us add that a modern person must obviously look for the answers to his questions wherever he or she chooses. Anthroposophy regards itself as *one* way among others that is open to everyone today within the framework of a new culture of questioning, which is indeed demanded of us in the present cultural epoch. A characteristic of this anthroposophical path is to put special emphasis on the need for raising our consciousness in the proper manner so as not to fall back into out-dated methods. The development of the consciousness soul involves to begin with a huge step in humanity towards self-reliance. Spiritual substance which was in earlier times couched in customs, traditions and religious forms is fast disappearing, and human beings have to learn to live in a kind of inner vacuum. As we saw in the life of Parzival, who had to go through *dullness* and *doubt,* we find ignorance, doubt, a feeling of the senselessness of our existence and deepest loneliness as the attendant phenomena of a new light that can arise in the innermost heart[65] of liberated human beings if they are really and truly searching. Finding oneself as an ego means initially separation, and ego fulfilment is the rediscovery of the world and one's fellow human beings. As we indicated in the very first chapter, the awakening Imagination is a bridge; it is the rediscovery, the reawakening, of Isis-Sophia, who has been locked up in the glass coffin of human consciousness.

> We must find our way back again; we must rediscover the possibility of enabling the inner core of things, which today is merely abstract mathematics, to be intensified into the picture life of Imagination...
>
> We must realize that Isis, the living, divine Sophia, had to be lost ... We shall, however, also realize that when living Imagination is awakened out of the dead field of mathematics, kinematics and geometry this is the finding of Isis, the finding of the new Isis, the divine Sophia, whom human beings must find if the Christ force which they have possessed since the Mystery of Golgotha is to become fully alive, that is, filled through and through with the light of purest awareness.[66]

This is something that concerns everybody in our time, whatever his or her professional calling. And the capacity to form Imaginations is there, potentially, in every human being. One can candidly say that in no other period of human history have people longed for pictures as much as they do in our civilization. We are constantly surrounded by them! The hundreds of illustrated papers and film strips of every kind that flood the market, the renewed interest in fairy-tale and fantasy literature we can observe in recent years, the whole field of advertising placards, and not least the screenlike nature of our towns, point like a seismograph to important movements and impulses in the subconscious of present-day humanity. Related to this is the phenomenon of the New Age complex of recent years with its search for holistic experience and an expansion of consciousness. People have the urge, today, whether they know it or not, to break through the limitations of their ordinary thinking and actions, for a new age has dawned. There is great danger, however, that individually people will fail to hear the inner voice calling for an intensification of ego consciousness, or will drown it with cheap substitutes that could lead to unforeseeable consequences.

This is a very delicate point, for on the one hand everyone should be free to choose for themselves where they want to look for their answers. That is a basic principle of our time. On the other hand we live according to quite definite evolutionary demands. History depicts an organic growth and maturing of humanity. Just as a growing child should neither remain stuck in his childhood nor anticipate what belongs to a much later time, although both are possible, every individual of our time must ask themselves whether what they are doing meets up to the demands of the Time Spirit. A great many phenomena today point to the fact that far more energetic strides in the direction of Imagination are necessary for everybody's good, for substitutes are there to excess. Besides the untransformed intellect, which is still being exclusively cultivated in our educational establishments, there are two powerful hindrances barring the way to the sphere of imaginative consciousness:

the perpetual exposure to the audio-visual mass media, and anachronistic paths of meditation and their practice. We shall now make a short survey to show what we mean by this, and I ask you to bear in mind what was said in the first chapter regarding some of the characteristics of imaginative consciousness, especially its creative-dynamic momentum and the central importance of the ego in the whole process. It was also mentioned that Imagination is capable of grasping the spiritual part of nature.

An imaginative picture is built up logically and harmoniously and leads to an experience of wholeness that brings about on the one hand a strengthening of one's own life forces and on the other hand awakens the kind of lively enthusiasm which arises because one is slowly beginning to be aware of the true meaning of the world.

There dawns on one the force 'which binds the world and guides its course'. The ego grows stronger and expands. One is well aware of coming closer to a spiritual being, and this can be like a first experience of communion and is a foretaste of the depths of inspirational and intuitive knowledge. I mentioned before that Imagination, Inspiration and Intuition are causally connected. It is worth noting the way Imaginations first appear. All the different parts arise as though simultaneously and then disappear again straight away, so that ordinary memory is of no use. One must always 'recreate' them anew.

If we compare this with television, and look at the nature of the pictures and the way they function, we experience a clear caricature of the stages of Imagination.

A picture is not first built up by the ego but called up *in* the person by the medium. The level of wakefulness of the average television watcher is lower than the normal state.[67] One has no control over these pictures, whose sequence is disconnected. For instance, we see the inside of a room and then are suddenly on the high seas, and then perhaps suddenly in a car, and so on, the hectic nature of the pictures reaching a climax in the innumerable advertisement flashes that are continually being sent out. The debility and tiredness one feels after watching television for a while shows that our life forces were really being undermined. Nevertheless, television always holds a strong fascination and people want more and more of it. They are often under the impression, especially when there are live transmissions, that their consciousness is being widened. They are more intensely connected with events than through the press. I am seeing this in common with millions of other people.

I have the chance of sharing the sorrows and joys of a whole nation. This can arouse a more or less conscious feeling of a kind of communion with vast sections of humanity and subliminally can take on the features of a feeling of wholeness.

The kind of manipulation this can often bring about, in the direction of group opinions among other things, is of course difficult to put one's finger on to begin with. It was the media philosopher Marshall McLuhan who pointed to this aspect of media absorption. McLuhan expounds that the media are 'extensions of particular human abilities—be they psychological or physical'.[68]

> Film and television complete the circle of mechanizing the human senses. With an omnipresent ear and a mobile eye we have destroyed writing, that specialized acoustic-visual metaphor which created the energy of western civilization. By superseding writing we are regaining our *wholeness*—not at a national or cultural level but on a cosmic one ... We are beginning once more to structure our primal feelings and emotions from which the alphabet has separated us for 3,000 years.[69]

On another occasion he speaks in this connection of a new age, an 'all-at-once-world', in which everything vibrates with everything else in a comprehensive electric field ... the entire human family will be welded together into one comprehensive membrane.'

It is very instructive that he finally connects the world of Christian Mysteries, the Whitsun miracle and the Christ Himself with the whole complex of the media and cosmic consciousness mentioned above: 'Today computers hold out the promise of a means of instant translation of any code or language into any other code or language. The computer, in short, promises by technology a Pentacostal condition of universal understanding and unity. The next logical step would seem to be not to translate but to bypass languages in favour of a general cosmic consciousness...' And on another occasion: 'In a Christian sense that is merely a new interpretation of the mystical body of Christ; and Christ is after all the furthest extension of a human being.'

This is demonstrably the counter-image of what Imagination is able to give. And a person who constantly exposes himself to the media is manipulated and loses his identity, instead of becoming newly born in his ego and opening himself to the world through his awakening imaginative consciousness in freedom and love. Again it was McLuhan who formulated this in a very drastic way: 'When people live in an electronic environment their whole nature becomes changed and their identity amalgamates with a collective whole. They become one of a herd.'[70]

These are all aspects that have to be looked at with discrimination, of course, for not every television viewer loses his ego. But these observations cannot be just swept aside. It must be said that from the aspect of an increase in the forces of a person's fantasy, which is the native soil of real Imagination, frequent viewing of television—and judging by the phenomenon of television addiction this can unfortunately even be seen in children—kills off just those organs of comprehension by means of which a person is aware of meaning in the world and of the setting of new objectives.

Young people in particular bring with them into earthly happenings experiences and aims gathered in pre-natal worlds, and what they especially bring are imaginative forces from the

spheres in which both human beings and the world in reality
come into being and are maintained. Where education is
concerned young people ought to be provided with teaching
methods and subject matter that do justice to this fundamental
part of their nature. The element of art, even from the point of
view of a tool for teaching, should pervade our whole education. Rudolf Steiner in particular, whose own education was in
science, never grew tired of urging the necessity of bringing
'pictures into the whole life of culture', pictures such as are
demanded by the laws of human evolution.[71]

In what sense he wanted this to be understood can be seen
from the following quotations:

> Now we must clearly understand ... that we bring down from
> the spiritual world, at least in the form of effects, what we have
> experienced in this spiritual world. When we move in ordinary
> life from one locality to another we take with us not only our
> clothes but also our soul-spiritual belongings. In like manner
> one brings along into this world through conception and birth
> the consequences and effects of what has been undergone in the
> spiritual world. In the period of time which mankind has just
> been living through, concerning which we know that it began
> around the middle of the fifteenth century AD, a human being,
> through his spirit-soul entity, brought along forces of the soul
> devoid of images, forces containing no pictures ... It is for this
> reason that above everything else the life of intellect has arisen
> and flourished ... This explains the slight inclination mankind
> had for developing original creations of fantasy since the
> middle of the fifteenth century. Fantasy is in truth only a
> terrestrial reflection of super-earthly Imagination ... And now
> the age begins—and in many respects this is the real reason for
> the stormy character of our times—in which the souls who
> descend through conception and birth into earthly life bring
> along for themselves images from the spiritual world ... Now it
> is generally true that humanity resists the images indwelling in
> the astral body, images experienced prior to conception.[72] In a
> way, human beings repel what ought to find its way out of the
> depths of their being into the astral body ... There are dry,

prosaic people who would really like to exclude any education by means of fairy-tales, legends or anything illuminated by imagination. In our Waldorf School system we have made it our priority that the lessons of the children entering primary school will proceed from pictorial descriptions, from the life-filled presentation of images, from elements taken from legends and fairy-tales. Even what the children are initially meant to learn about the nature and processes of the animal kingdom, the plant and the mineral kingdoms, should not be expressed in a dry, matter-of-fact manner. It should be clothed in imaginative, legendary, fairy-talelike elements. For seated deep within the child's soul are the Imaginations that have been received in the spiritual world. They seek to come to the surface. And the teacher adopts the right attitude towards the children if he presents them with pictures. By placing images before the children's souls there flash up from their souls those images or, strictly speaking, those forces of pictorial presentation which have been received before birth or, let us say, prior to conception.

...the young person possesses forces in his body that will burst out elsewhere if they are not brought to the surface in pictorial presentation. What will be the result of modern mistaken education? These forces do not become lost; they spread out, gain existential ground, and invade the thoughts, feelings and impulses of the will. And what kind of people will come into being from that? They will be rebels, revolutionaries, dissatisfied people; people who do not know what they want.

...If the world is in a state of revolt today, it is really Heaven that is revolting, which means the Heaven that is held back in the souls of men which then comes to the fore not in its own form but in its opposite—in strife and bloodshed instead of Imaginations. No wonder that the individuals who destroy the social fabric actually have the feeling that they are doing good. For what do they sense in themselves? They feel Heaven within themselves; only it assumes the form of a caricature in their soul. This is how serious the truths are that we must comprehend today.

It is in the same sense as this that we have to look on the

effect the media have of undermining free fantasy, as was indicated above in the case of television.

In this connection the practice of art assumes great importance. It should play a far more active part in our everyday lives than it does today, for in art—as already mentioned—those Sophia forces are at work that sustain and further every kind of creative, imaginative endeavour. Art, whether it is being created or merely just experienced has, not only for children but for everybody, a formative and therapeutic effect that can re-enliven many a thing today that is being constantly impaired, not least of all by exposure to the media.

Imagination is a faculty that is meant to be developed gradually on a worldwide scale and added to our normal thinking consciousness.[73] In a way, the world of electronic images is anticipating this stage of cognition, and we are bound to call it materialistic anachronism. In this sense it presents one of the biggest hindrances to attaining imaginative consciousness.

The second hindrance, as mentioned at the beginning of this chapter—we shall restrict ourselves to two important aspects only of this multi-layered problem—is concerned in the main with something that comes from the distant past but which offers something that is in keeping with the times. We mean all the practices of extended consciousness which, essentially, require and promote an antiquated, pre-intellectual, passive-receptive state of mind, whether they are so-called 'youth sects' or presentable centres of meditation. And these are legion.

Not all these paths lead to visionary experiences, which are dangerous because the awakeness of the ego is concerned, as is for instance often the case with the apparently more modern-seeming autogenic training; some of them even make a direct attack on the sphere of Inspiration. A person is supposed to become a mere mouthpiece, a 'channel' of the guiding spiritual powers. The real aim of these beings is seen in the very manner in which they make their way into people, so that by means of 'messages' they can direct a group of meditants their way.

Instead of the ego-force of the striving human being increasing in spiritual strength in order to reach the spiritual sphere in a responsible manner, the ego makes way for a higher power just as in ancient Egypt the Pharoah was the mouthpiece of the gods. Think of the famous statue of Pharoah Chephren in the Cairo Museum. The king is seated, and behind his head the Horus falcon, an image of the Sun god, spreads his wings over him to protect and guide him. That was a pre-ego stage of evolution and therefore deeply justified at that time, but not today. Now it cannot mean anything else but the giving up of a person's most precious possession, the creative ego, which is called to attain spiritual knowledge by way of the greatest possible inner dynamic[74] and not merely receive it in the form of 'messages'. Such practices are rooted in devastating anachronism, even though they are presumed to be carried out with the best of intentions. For a person's dependency on these misanthropic forces continues even after death, when he has laid aside his bodily sheath. One has associated oneself with their activity, and one unites oneself spiritually with that with which one has an affinity. So it is not only the developing of independent Imaginations that is adversely affected but also the capacity for independent Inspirations, which exists potentially in every human being. Bear in mind what was said in this connection in the first chapter.

To illustrate this point I shall cite the following voice that is alleged to come from the 'heavenly Father' and was revealed through a person with mediumistic ability:

> Let not your heart be troubled. You believe in Me. Trust in Me. Allow no doubts or fears to enter. Let yourself be used as My channel to radiate My love at all times. Step out of that mist of despondency into pure light where all is clear and beauty

surrounds you ... You are inclined to forget the way that millions live in the big cities, the hustle and bustle, the rat race, the dirt and squalor. It is good to remember this, because it will fill your heart with deep gratitude that I have led you to this life where peace and beauty surround you, where the air is pure and the living is simple. You are mightily blessed. Accept these blessings, stretch out and do My work, and let My peace and love be yours at all times, gifts from Me, your heavenly Father. Always go with My guidance and never against it. It is when you go against it that trouble starts. I am very patient and very loving and keep on showing you the way. But it is up to you to take it ... You are not living as individuals but as a group. Therefore you can find perfect unity only if you seek My will. It will be a very thrilling and exciting life for all of you, but you must stay close to Me and not try to run things your way.[75]

Gurus may also work in this way if they want, through their own egos, to have such an influence on the souls of their adherents that they can rule them. Bhagwan Shree Rajneesh, known later as 'Osho', is no longer living but his works are of great symptomatic importance in this context. Apart from the fact that the movement he inaugurated, or rather his work, still exists, it is typical of the endeavours of similar trends. Here are a few examples among many: 'Forget your ego. Be like trees in the wind.' 'If you let go and become a part of the current, it will be easier ... Extinguish yourselves whilst you are here with me...' 'If you swing a torch round quickly in circles, it gives the illusion of a wheel of fire. Your thoughts go round in a circle like this and create the illusion of an ego. Slow your thoughts down until you finally stop them—and the wheel of fire, your ego, disappears.' 'Things gradually become clear to one and one eventually relaxes; bit by bit you let your ego go and I enter more and more deeply into you. And then, one day, without any warning, it has happened. All of a sudden you realize it has happened. Now my light shines in your being, now my heart beats in your breast.' Satyananda, one of Bhagwan's disciples, adds: 'Bhagwan has already said twice in lectures that Teertha [one of his colleagues] is no longer separate from existence—a man without an ego. Bhagwan therefore gave out that he could work directly through Teertha. Teertha was a "hollow bamboo pipe".'[76]

We see clearly here that the independent ego is being undermined. As unspiritual as it may seem on the one hand, it is irreplaceable on the other hand as the principle for our inner independence. Without the ego—which we have to transform and not do away with—there could be no knowledge of a spiritual kind such as is needed in our time. Bhagwan could certainly bring about all sorts of states of intoxication, and there are surely all kinds of 'ecstasies' and 'raptures' also attainable along other occult paths, even 'states of bliss',[77] yet these serve only to increase a person's own pleasure and are clearly distinguishable from the chaste qualities of real Imagination. We are, of course, talking of experiences that are not always bound to have the kind of visionary character we have described, even if they are—as is the case with Imagination—'bodyfree' experiences; the Greek *ék-stasis* means, of course, 'going out of oneself'. We brought these examples primarily in connection with our concern for the ego.

Imaginations can certainly be felt very deeply, but never ecstatically or rapturously even when the spectrum of feelings can on some occasions reach quite new levels of intensity—for the ego is present and influences the process. The kind of communion we spoke of, which arises through interaction, depends on the *expansion* of our most individual ego forces and not on being *possessed*. It is in this sense too that we must understand the words of Paul 'not I but the Christ in me' (see Chapter 3), for the human ego and the Christ Ego are woven out of the same light. Here we see the law of spiritual transparency again. Where our theme is concerned we have to draw a clear dividing line with regard to such practices.

So-called 'astral projection' too—when the soul moves about outside the body[78]—may be very sensational. Yet it does not give creative-imaginative insights into a real spiritual world, even if it does seem to open up new dimensions. As a rule it is the result of a separating off of the soul forces attached to the *physical* sense organization, and these work like a second bodily sheath which can pass through walls and move at tremendous speed through space. Experiences of this kind show a strange mixture of dream and physical reality. When it takes place on 'higher levels of vibration' it has, in so far as anything is 'seen', the typical anthropomorphic character of atavistic clairvoyance. This is connected with a projection or shift of the forces of perception in the physical-material body in areas to which only spiritualized forces of consciousness should have access. Whether such 'travellers' are conscious of it or not, they are trying to enter the spiritual world by the back-door so to speak—yet in reality they remain stuck at the threshold. When all is said and done, even with this method of training, which has great appeal to many people, the genuinely spiritual dimension of humanity and the world remains closed. The Christ-Sophia forces of a new, really body-free Imagination will not unfold that way.

In the tension between the forces working by means of the audio-visual media right into our subconscious and the forces activated through human mediums or out-of-date paths of meditation and other practices lies the field where the people of today, in striving to transform their intellect, are on the way to Imagination. It is a battle requiring both courage and energy because, to quote Paul, we wrestle not 'against flesh and blood, but against principalities, against powers, against the rulers of the darkness of this world, against spiritual wickedness in high places'.[79] In connection with Isis-Sophia I have described how imaginative consciousness does not see 'forces' only but beings, and these beings live in a quite definite spiritual sphere both within and outside human beings and play a part in the evolution of humanity. Thus in anthroposophy, as I have indicated, we speak of Ahriman and Lucifer as group spirits of a multitude of higher and lower entities.[80] Ahriman, the cold spirit of intellectual hardening, functions as, among other things, a cosmic force in every process of compression and solidification. In human thinking he stands for the lifeless, formally abstract element and, even though this gives strength and firmness to thinking, it is nevertheless fundamentally incapable of grasping life processes. He is the instigator of all necessary and unnecessary technical apparatus, and his sphere also infiltrates the mass media. His aim is to bring mankind things, in 'ahrimanized' form, that belong in the future. Lucifer, among other things, the lord of all self-centred conditions of ecstasy and intoxication, is likewise a cosmic power and functions in every kind of process of dissolution. In contrast to Ahriman, formlessness is his element. He is the instigator of all the subjective capriciousness in the ego. He wants above all to turn what is past, anachronistic and atavistic, by means of a kind of historic nostalgia, into something presentable and real. These are the forces we have to contend with. We do not have the slightest intention to paint the phenomena described in this chapter as devils, for in reality they do ultimately in many ways belong to human evolution. However, we shall get on top of them solely with the help of higher levels of cognition and a new morality acquired in the process, especially with regard to the already very advanced ahrimanization of our civilization:

> We cannot halt mechanization, for civilization has to go this way. Civilization requires ahrimanization. But it has to be accompanied by that which is now working its way to the surface from man's inner being, the wisdom, beauty and strength that man's inner being draws forth through the power of Imagination. For the worlds which will then arise will be worlds related to man, the kind of worlds that will have a spiritual and soul presence, while all around us the forces of ahrimanic machinery run their course. And the power arising out of Imagination, Inspiration and Intuition will be capable of controlling the things that would otherwise overpower human beings, in the maddening tempo of their ahrimanized environment. That which comes from the spiritual world by way of

Imagination, Inspiration and Intuition is stronger than all the horse-power years that may still arise from the mechanization of the world. Human beings would, however, be themselves overcome by the forces of mechanization if they were not to find a counterbalance to them, which they can indeed find in the revelations from the spiritual world, but these they have to strive for.

... If human beings mechanize the world around them through external science then it is all the more necessary that they get an inner science, a new wisdom, to arise out of their inner being. This will possess the strength to control that which would otherwise overwhelm them.[81]

We indicated in the first pages of this chapter that a new age had dawned. We stated that the awakening of 'living Imagination ... means the finding of Isis ... the divine Sophia, whom human beings have to find if the essence of Christ bestowed on us with the Mystery of Golgotha is to become alive in us, fully alive, that is, filled with light of purest awareness.' This new age, this new impulse in our human evolution, comes in conjunction with a new revelation of the Christ-Sophia forces both in human beings and in the cosmos. The developing of Imagination in our time is deeply connected with this. We can recognize it as a further metamorphosis of the stream flowing forth from Golgotha. In this sense 'we must learn to look up to the new Isis, to the holy Sophia, in the same way as the Egyptian looked from their Osiris to Isis. Christ's reappearance in spiritual form in the course of the twentieth century will not be solely an external occurrence but will happen only if human beings find the impulse represented by the holy Sophia.'[82]

Here we find once again the Whitsun union of the two aspects of the cosmic-earthly Sophia: living Imagination as a new form of wisdom gives birth to a new human being within the awakening Christ consciousness. Here we touch on the sphere that in anthroposophy is called 'Spirit Self'. And the numerous attacks against the forces of Imagination struggling to arise in every individual today are, ultimately, a battle against the Christ-Sophia, i.e. against the truly human element that aspires to manifest today in the course of a progressive evolution. This is why our present world situation is so serious.

Apocalypse Now:
Sophia and Babylon
The Reappearance of Christ

Particularly in the year 1910, and many times afterwards, Rudolf Steiner spoke from various points of view of the second coming of Christ in the etheric, in the spiritual sphere of purest life forces which can be reached by an imaginative consciousness acquired through training.[83] In this connection he also spoke of an initial hunchlike natural clairvoyance which will appear to begin with in individual people and grow in the course of our age into a faculty possessed by the whole of humanity—if they want to develop it further.

This clairvoyance, or rather these individual clairvoyant experiences, when a person is as it were surprised by sudden insight into the spiritual aspect of the Earth and of humanity, is certainly not the sort of negative occurrence referred to earlier. It is ordained by destiny and is not as a rule repeated. One gets the impression such experiences are meant as a clarion call to wake the person up and get him to change his way of life. Often they are fragile imaginative impressions which can be accompanied by a genuine inspirational factor, or they are even pure Inspirations.

The author has experienced such things himself. They are modern Damascus experiences and can occur both 'within' as well as 'outside', for in reality they belong to a higher, undivided dimension. Or according to the constitution and inner maturity of the person, they can sometimes be really 'dense', that is, they can appear as a physical phenomenon. However, the important thing is that they always leave one free to do as one likes about them. This is an infallible sign of their authenticity. Other examples are faint memories of a pre-birth existence or premonitions of the future. Something they all have in common is that they break through the categories of space and time. A layer of the soul is uncovered, and fully conscious Imagination can develop from this if the person has the will. It is of great significance to know that Lucifer and Ahriman are as it were on the look-out for such experiences. Lucifer whispers, among other things, that one has just experienced the deepest truths, and that one is considerably more highly developed than other people, and Ahriman strains himself to the utmost to prove that it was all shallow make-believe. The two of them can lead one either to illusions about one's own maturity or to despair over one's own state of soul. Their activity is as a rule so subtle that one hardly notices it. Therefore the greatest vigilance is necessary.

Whenever these budding faculties occur they should be understood, protected and nursed.

Rudolf Steiner explained how a spiritual training can help these forces to develop.

> These clairvoyant faculties can be acquired ever so much better by means of what we call esoteric schooling. However, because human beings are progressing, the very first beginnings of this will arise as a spontaneous, natural manifestation in humanity.
> ... Changes of this kind are going to happen in the human soul. A faculty that can be called etheric sight will occur. What is this connected with? Well, the Being we call the Christ lived once in the flesh on Earth at the beginning of our era. He will not come again in a physical body, for that was a unique event. However, the Christ will come again in etheric form ... Therefore human beings will have to grow to the level where they can perceive the Christ. For the statement of Christ, 'I am with you always, until the end of Earth days,' is the truth.[84]

Thus two things are connected with this faculty: an imaginative capacity that will to begin with be of the nature of a general feeling, a new light of consciousness for an entirely new world, and the experience of its centre, the Sun Logos, the Christ. It is just this image of the Sun that will illustrate for us the relation of Sophia to the Christ: Sophia is the light, as it were, the aura of Christ, and He appears within it like the activating centre of a totally new beginning in the development of humanity and the world. The birth of imaginative consciousness is also the birth of Sophia-Christ in the human being, the Christ presenting a concentration of the entire ego force of humanity since the creation—as was apparent to Moses in the burning bush—and Sophia the light of the soul, the light of consciousness within the cosmos, and both of them, now together, representing the power of cosmic-earthly resurrection.

The Whitsun Mystery happenings of the Grail have now become the concern of all humanity. This is an event of utmost significance!

Human beings are part of this centre, this new cosmos that is already starting to become visible through the cosmic-earthly activity of Christ-Sophia in our century. This reappearance is at the same time the first glimmer of light of a new Earth beginning; it is the dawn of the 'heavenly Jerusalem', as John in his Apocalypse calls the further development of that which began at Easter on Golgotha. He speaks in images that apply also to our present time and call on our deepest feelings of responsibility. This is how he describes this future picture of the Earth:

> And I saw a new heaven and a new earth: for the first heaven and the first earth were passed away; and there was no more sea. And I, John, saw the holy city, new Jerusalem, coming down from God out of heaven, prepared as a bride adorned for her husband. And I heard a great voice out of heaven saying:
>
> Behold, the tabernacle of God is with men, and he will dwell with them, and they shall be his people, and God himself shall be with them and be their God. And God shall wipe away all tears from their eyes; and there shall be no more death, neither sorrow, nor crying, neither shall there be any more pain: for the former things are passed away.

> And he that sat upon the throne said, Behold, I make all things new![85]

This is, of course, the image of a very far future, yet the most important factors for this are already being set in train in our time—for man is called to take part consciously in this process. He is as it were the first actor of a tremendously dramatic happening taking place within and around him. Let us look at an earlier passage of the Apocalypse:

> And there appeared a great wonder in heaven; a woman clothed with the sun, and the moon under her feet, and upon her head a crown of twelve stars: And she being with child cried, travailing in birth, and pained to be delivered.
>
> And there appeared another wonder in heaven; and behold a great red dragon having seven heads and ten horns, and seven crowns upon his heads. And his tail drew the third part of the stars of heaven, and did cast them to the earth, and the dragon stood before the woman which was ready to be delivered, for to devour her child as soon as it was born. And she brought forth a man child, who was to rule all nations with a brazen rod: and her child was caught up unto God, and to his throne. And the woman fled into the wilderness, where she hath a place prepared of God.
>
> ... And there was a war in heaven: Michael and his angels fought against the dragon, and the dragon fought and his angels, and prevailed not; neither was there place found any more in heaven. And the great dragon was cast out, that old serpent, called the Devil, and Satan, which deceiveth the whole world: he was cast out into the earth, and his angels were cast out with him.[86]

If we try to understand the language of these pictures we can arrive at the following, always assuming that pictures which refer to the supersensible realm can be interpreted on many levels.[87] The images of the Apocalypse also describe at one and the same time great spans of time or processes, and therefore they can partly apply to the present day. They encompass dimensions that are at the same time both within the human soul and in the outer world. What takes place spiritually in the world can be perceived within man and what occurs in the depths of the human soul can be rediscovered as world content. Present and future events are continuously inter-weaving.

It is in dimensions such as these that we see the image of the Sophia. The shining circle of twelve stars round her head gives expression to her cosmic power. The overcoming of dead matter, now in the form of dross, is shown in the moon beneath her feet. In the middle of this tension between the upper and the lower realm there arises, woven out of pure Sun forces, a new human being whose ego principle, which surpasses all national distinctions, appears as an upright brazen rod. The 'woman' is an archetypal picture of the birth pangs of a new age of mankind. The dragon, representing a combination of Lucifer and Ahriman, as the bearer of all the hindrances to evolution, wants to corrupt this new ego principle, that is, to make it part of himself. However, the Archangel Michael liberates 'Heaven' by hurling the adver-saries down to the Earth, meaning that they are now active in the human realm, and that is where they have to be overcome. This frees the sphere of the spirit where our true self—the new human being—can be sought.

Our gaze is now drawn to the inner aspect of human nature, the other scene of this event. New forces have to be acquired. The dragon pursued the Sophia being who has now become the human soul, but she is given 'two wings of a great eagle', which we recognize to be an organ of Imagination, the two-petalled lotus flower.[88] In the solitude of the desert—an image of the developmental conditions of the consciousness soul—there is the opportunity for her to assert herself. The flood of water that came towards her out of the jaws of the dragon is not able to destroy her: the ego-nature of the consciousness soul is aided by the forces of the Persephone-imbued Earth, for the wings of the eagle have restored to the soul its cosmic nature and the flood of anti-ego forces no longer has power over her. In the words of the Apocalypse:

> And when the dragon saw that he was cast unto the earth, he persecuted the woman which brought forth the man child. And to the woman were given two wings of a great eagle that she might fly into the wilderness, into her place, where she was nourished for a time, and times, and half a time, from the face of the serpent. And the serpent cast out of his mouth water as a flood after the woman, that he might cause her to be carried away of the flood. And the earth helped the woman, and the earth opened her mouth, and swallowed up the flood which the dragon cast out of his mouth. And the dragon was wrath with the woman.[89]

This battle is already taking place today in every person of our time. The dangers mentioned in the previous chapter are an absolute part of this. We must remember that the Apocalypse contains *archetypal images* of the evolution of humanity, and that the concrete form they will take on will vary according to the epoch in which they manifest. Therefore it is permissible to refer in this connection to the world of electronically produced pictures and the crippling effect these have on the activity of the ego, even though the Apocalypse was written well before they were foreseen. The telling factor is that it is an endangering of the ego by the 'dragon', as is also the case with anachronisms along the paths of occult training.

In the final analysis we are, at the present time, caught up in a battle for the individual human soul, which will be a long one. Christ-Sophia and the Archangel Michael—the great protector of human beings on their hard path to the Grail—live and work in a way that leaves the individual free to find his true path.[90] The adversaries, the 'seducers of the whole of mankind' are also unremittingly active, and they know through which doors they can force their way into us, namely, through Sophia-Achamod—as the part of the soul that participated in the Fall of Man into the realm of egoism and desires was called in the days of the spirit knowledge of early Christianity.[91]

On our way towards becoming fully human we lost long ago our original cosmic innocence and purity. Sophia is both the origin and the goal of our inner development. What she has to become is the essence of the present, the being of our time. What we have to do is to bring light and transformation to 'Achamod', that dark part of our soul—as Parzival did—for then it will become one with the Sophia and give birth to a new human being within us who, already today, can be aware of the new Earth of light. In this unredeemed part of our soul there is also a cosmic principle at work; however, it is a counter-image of the Sophia. It is the spirit being whom the writer of the Apocalypse describes in the image of the 'Whore Babylon'.[92]

Wherever a human being's *thinking*, on its quest for the riddles of existence, can become transparent for the spirit in both humanity and the cosmos, this other being tries to cloud it and imprison it either in materialistic self-conceit or in arrogant intellectual self-admiration. *Feeling* shall not have a selfless relation to the environment but become hardened in self-centredness and complacency; and lastly, under her influence the *will* shall not become an organ for noble human goals but solely a means to self-satisfaction through the exercise of power and through the craving for things of a purely physical and material kind. Present-day sexuality also belongs here in so far as it has not yet acquired the dignity of true and undivided love as demonstrated in the inner relationship between Parzival and Conduiramour.[93]

All these examples represent a violent *corrupting of egohood* in the process of which one can also see the working of a third power for evil, so that in all we see a counter-image to the Trinity, as was briefly sketched in Chapter 3.

Rudolf Steiner calls the bearers of this third power the 'Asuras', and

...they will generate evil with a far mightier force than was wielded by the satanic powers ... or by the luciferic spirits.

... For these asuric beings will prompt what has been seized
hold of by them, namely, the very core of man's being, the
consciousness soul together with the 'I', to unite with earthly
materiality. Fragment after fragment will be torn out of the 'I',
and in the same measure in which the asuric spirits establish
themselves in the consciousness soul man must leave part of his
existence behind on the Earth. What thus becomes the prey of
the asuric powers will be irretrievably lost. Not that the whole
man need become their victim, but parts of his spirit will be
torn away by the asuric powers. These asuric powers are
heralded today by the prevailing tendency to live wholly in the
material world and to be oblivious of the reality of spiritual
beings and spiritual worlds.

... And in many things that need not be further characterized
here, many things that in the big cities come to expression in
orgies of dissolute sensuality, we can already perceive the lurid,
hellish glare of the spirits we call the Asuras.[94]

As a part of this phenomenon there are two aspects of
today's culture that mount a very strong attack on human
egos, as can easily be identified through the effects they have:
drugs[95] and alcohol.[96] Although these factors are a problem
enough in themselves, when we look at them in conjunction
with higher stages of knowledge and with the birth of Christ
within man they acquire a new dimension that is just as much
part of a characterization of our time. And we can take a very
positive view of the fact that more and more is being done
today to come to grips with these threats. Seen in this light the
Whore Babylon can indeed appear as a 'feminine' centre of
anti-Christian forces or beings. Coming to terms with
Achamod-Babylon is an inseparable part of today's battle for
the Imagination and the new birth of man. The corresponding
passage in the Apocalypse says:

And there came one of the seven angels which had the seven
vials, and talked with me saying unto me, Come hither! I will
show unto thee the judgment of the great whore that sitteth

upon many waters: with whom the kings of the earth have committed fornication, and the inhabitants of the earth have been made drunk with the wine of her fornication. So he carried me away in the spirit into the wilderness: and I saw a woman sit upon a scarlet coloured beast, full of names of blasphemy, having seven heads and ten horns. And the woman was arrayed in purple and scarlet colour, and decked with gold and precious stones and pearls, having a golden cup in her hand full of abominations and filthiness of her fornication. And upon her forehead was a name written, a mystery:

Babylon the Great, the mother of harlots and abomination of the earth.

...And he saith unto me, The waters which thou sawest, where the whore sitteth, are peoples, and multitudes...[97]

This last image of the waters complements our description of the workings of the anti-Sophia forces. The 'shepherd of all nations with the brazen rod', the full ego-human being (he who has outgrown everything of a nationalistic nature) shall not be born, but instead the herdlike human being, who falls back, among other things, into racism and nationalism, as can be seen time and time again in our century, and not for the last time. Babylon with the golden cup full of abominations is in the last instance a counter-image of the Grail. What she can bring to birth within man is only the anti-Christ.

Whether it be the mass media or atavisms, mere sexuality or drugs, alcohol or intellectualism, what we have on our hands in our time is a battle for the Imagination on the largest possible scale. Over and against this, however, Michael and his hosts, the Christ and Sophia, are at work in a manner that engenders enormous forces in human beings, so that in course of time evil can gradually be transformed and redeemed. This process begins in individuals, will then extend to the social environment and finally to the Earth itself.

When the clarity of formal thinking becomes impregnated with the life blood of Imagination the redemption of Ahriman can begin. When, as a consequence of this, the feeling soul again becomes chaste, Lucifer will be redeemed, and the sting can be taken out of the workings of the Asuras when the shepherd with the brazen rod within us, the Christ-Sophia human being, becomes social reality.

On the one hand we certainly feel the greatest concern in the face of the power wielded by Achamod-Babylon in the world of today, yet on the other hand there is a picture corresponding to that reality that can *also* be experienced today, when our eyes of Imagination are brought slowly towards the light. Within a rainbow aura there arises, like a mighty sunrise, the Sophia-Christ Earth of light, interwoven with all the deeds of wisdom, beauty and love which mankind has up to now been able to wring from the adversaries. Just as the body of Christ passed through death, our Earth will also pass to an ever greater extent through a transformation, so that one day the new Jerusalem, 'The bride of the Lamb', shall become full reality. Babylon shall then also be overcome. Even if today our civilization appears from some aspects to be in ruins, this picture can give each individual, in their Parzival-like struggles, in their questioning and erring, the certainty that they are not alone. At the threshold of this *new* etheric Earth we find, as the silent protector and impulse-giver of all truly culture-renewing deeds of our time, the Archangel Michael, the strong Angel of the Apocalypse in our time.

Notes

Most of the passages from Rudolf Steiner's works quoted in this book arose as verbal communication not intended for publication. His audiences consisted as a rule of people whom Rudolf Steiner could count on to have already become acquainted with extensive areas of anthroposophically orientated spiritual science. This explains his manner and approach. The author of this work has endeavoured so to include these passages in his text that they can be understood in their setting without giving the impression of being out of context.

('GA' stands for *Gesamtausgabe*, the collected works of Rudolf Steiner in the original German. His books and published lectures are available in English from Rudolf Steiner Press, Bristol, and Anthroposophic Press, New York.)

1 See for example Rudolf Steiner, *Occult Science, an Outline,* Rudolf Steiner Press 1984; *The Deed of Christ and the Opposing Spiritual Powers—Lucifer, Ahriman, Mephistopheles, Asuras,* Anthroposophic Press 1976. Lecture of 22 March 1909 in Berlin.
2 J.W. von Goethe, *Faust* 1, Night. Translated by Bayard Taylor.
3 See, for example, H. Rieche and W. Schuchhardt, *Zivilisation der Zukunft* (Civilization of the Future), Stuttgart 1981.
4 See Rudolf Steiner, *The Gospel of St John*, Anthroposophic Press 1984. Lecture 1 given on 30 May 1908 in Hamburg.
5 Rudolf Steiner, *Inner Impulses of Human Evolution*, Anthroposophic Press 1984. Lecture of 17 September 1916 in Dornach.
6 A quote from the edition of Konrad Sandkühler's translation of *Perceval* by Chrétien de Troyes, Stuttgart 1929.
7 Matthew 1:20 and following, and 2:12–15.
8 See Wilhelm Rath's introduction to *Alanus ab Insulis—Der Anticlaudian*, Stuttgart 1983.
9 See Rudolf Steiner, *Spiritual Guidance of the Individual and Humanity*, Anthroposophic Press, 1992, Chapter 2.
10 Brunetto Latini, *Tesoretto* (translated here from German into English), Stuttgart 1979.

11 Rudolf Steiner, *Einleitungen zu Goethes Naturwissenschaftlichen Schriften*, GA 1, 1987, Chapter 4.

12 Rudolf Steiner, *Anthroposophical Leading Thoughts*, Rudolf Steiner Press 1985, Thought No. 1.

13 Rudolf Steiner, *The Occult Significance of the Bhagavad Gita*, Anthroposophic Press, 1984. Lecture given on 29 May 1913 in Helsingfors.

14 Hermann Poppelbaum, *The Battle for a New Consciousness*, Mercury Press, New York 1993, p.43.

15 See for example C.G. Jung, *Erinnerungen, Träume, Gedanken* (Memories, Dreams, Thoughts), Zürich, Stuttgart 1967.

16 See for example the articles by Winfried Paarmann in *Das Goetheanum*, Dornach, 20 and 27 January 1985.

17 Rudolf Steiner, *Stages of Higher Knowledge*, Anthroposophic Press 1990.

18 Rudolf Steiner, *Occult Science, An Outline*, op. cit. Preface to the 20th Edition.

19 See Rudolf Steiner, *Stages of Higher Knowledge*, op. cit., chapters on Inspiration and Intuition. Also further exercises for the acquisition of imaginative consciousness in Paul Eugen Schiller, *Rudolf Steiner and Initiation. The Anthroposophical Path of Inner Schooling. A Survey*, Anthroposophic Press, chapter on the level of imaginative cognition.

20 Rudolf Steiner, *Theosophy of the Rosicrucians*, Rudolf Steiner Press 1981. Lecture of 25 May 1907 in Munich. This lecture cycle also contains a description of the different members of man's being. Also see Rudolf Steiner, *Occult Science, An Outline*.

21 See *Occult Science, An Outline*, op. cit., chapter: 'Knowledge of the Higher Worlds'.

22 See Rudolf Steiner, *Stages of Higher Knowledge*, op. cit., 'Inspiration and Intuition'. As distinct from this, with atavistic clairvoyance visions appeared as outer perceptions. It is important to remember when a person sees imaginatively he has to speak in pictures in order to make himself understood. This can lead to the erroneous conclusion that Imaginations are similar to sense perceptions in nature.

23 Rudolf Steiner, *Knowledge of the Higher Worlds. How is it Achieved?*, Rudolf Steiner Press 1989, chapter entitled 'Control of Thoughts and Feelings'.

24 See Rudolf Steiner, *Stages of Higher Knowledge*, op. cit. For the connection between the higher stages of knowledge and the human sense organs, see Rudolf Steiner, *Spiritual Science as a Foundation for Social Forms*, Anthroposophic Press and Rudolf Steiner Press 1986. Lecture of 8 August 1920 in Dornach.

25 See Rudolf Steiner, *Theosophy of the Rosicrucians*, op. cit. Lecture of 6 June 1907 in Munich.

26 Rudolf Steiner, 'Der Baugedanke des Goetheanum' (The Architectural Impulse of the Goetheanum), Rudolf Steiner Verlag, Dornach. Lecture of 29 June 1921 in Berne.

27 Rudolf Steiner, *The Challenge of Our Times*, Anthroposophic Press 1941. Lecture of 7 December 1918 in Dornach. The chief purpose for giving this quotation is to show the great importance of having a 'picture' of social life. The wooden sculpture of 'The Group' is one possible way mentioned in these lectures of arriving at impulses that can be effective in a social way (see illustration).

28 See Rudolf Steiner, *Anthroposophical Leading Thoughts*, op. cit., 'Human Freedom and the Michael Age'.

29 *Der Spiegel*, 13 June 1983, p.189. Schopper also refers to the aspect described here in an article with the characteristic title 'Die Grenzen unseres Weltbildes' (The Limits of Our World Picture) in *Bild der Wissenschaft*, Stuttgart 1991.

30 J.W. von Goethe, *Sprüche in Prosa* (Prose Aphorisms), Stuttgart 1967, Aphorisms 165 and 188.

31 Novalis, *Werke und Briefe* (Works and Letters), Munich 1968. From the fragments on cosmology and religion Nos 537 and 539.

32 Sigismund von Gleich, *Die Wahrheit als Gesamtumfang aller Weltansichten* (The Truth, Covering the Total Range of World Views), Stuttgart 1989, p.41 and following.

33 See J.W. von Goethe, *Sprüche in Prosa* (Prose Aphorisms), Stuttgart 1967, Aphorism 811.

34 Bernardus Silvestris, *De Mundi Universitate*, Stuttgart, no date. And see Wilhelm Rath's introduction to *Alanus ab Insulis—Der Anticlaudian*.

35 See also Hans Peter van Manen, 'The Anthroposophical Impulse in the Environmental Movement' in *Transparent Realities*, Temple Lodge Publishing, 1994; and Richard Karutz, *Maria im Fernen Osten—das Problem der Kuan Yin* (Mary in

the Far East—the Phenomenon of the Kuan Yin), Stuttgart 1930.

36 It is interesting and instructive to note that words in the mainly Latin-based Romance languages that have to do with thinking processes are identical with words in the realm of gynaecology. For instance, the Italian words for world conception are usually *concezione del mondo*, which means a conception by the being of the world.

37 Arthur Schult, *Maria-Sophia*, Bietigheim 1960, pp.23–26.

38 Rudolf Steiner, 'The Mysteries of the Orient and of Christianity.' Lecture of 5 February 1913 in Berlin. The following three quotations come from this lecture. It contains a detailed description of what is only briefly outlined here. To complement this, see also Rudolf Steiner, *Macrocosm and Microcosm*, Rudolf Steiner Press 1985. Lecture of 25 March 1910 in Vienna.

39 2 Genesis 3:12 and following.

40 See also Wolfgang Militz's study, in: *3000 Jahre Sonnengesänge—Ägyptische Mysterien* (3,000 Years of Songs to the Sun—Egyptian Mysteries), Stuttgart 1985, which gives a vivid description of the cultural climate of the Egyptian Isis civilization; and Wolfgang Greiner, *Gralsgeheimnisse* (Grail Mysteries), Dornach 1990.

41 Rudolf Steiner, *The Gospel of St Matthew*, Rudolf Steiner Press 1985. Lecture of 3 September 1910 in Berne. See also the essays by Sigismund von Gleich, in *Blätter für Anthroposophie*, Dornach 1951, Nos 1 and 5. (This periodical is no longer published.)

42 Sigismund von Gleich, *Blätter für Anthroposophie*, and in other places, No. 5, Note 41. He describes this process as follows:
1. 2100–1400 BC: via the physical body (since Abraham).
2. 1400–700 BC: via the etheric body (Moses lived around 1400).
3. 700 until the time of Jesus Christ: via the astral body.
4. From the time of Jesus Christ to 700 AD: via the sentient soul.
5. 700–1400 AD: via the intellectual soul.
6. 1400–2100 AD: via the consciousness soul, and possibly:
7. 2100–2800 AD: via the Spirit Self.
   See also Rudolf Grosse, *The Living Being Anthroposophia*, Chapter 5, Anthroposophic Press 1986.

43 Luke 3:21 and following. The translation of the New Testament used here and in the following quotations is the one by Kalmia Bittleston, Floris Books 1990.
44 John 1:24–34 (translation by Kalmia Bittleston).
45 Matthew 28:20.
46 See Karl König, *Swans and Storks*, Floris Books, 1979. Chapter: 'The Dove as a Sacred Bird'.
47 Paul to the Galatians 1:5 and 2:20. The connection between the female principle and the birth of 'the Christ in me' is also stressed by Rudolf Steiner: 'The "Holy Spirit" and the "Christ in us" are one and the same, but at different *stages of development*. One could also say that the "Holy Spirit" is the ... mother principle of the ... Son principle of Christ. It is by virtue of the development occurring in us out of the "Holy Spirit" (the Christ and the female creator) that we have the "Christ in us". For originally the "Holy Spirit" was none other than the Mother of God (Isis etc.).' Letter of 19 August 1902, in Volume 2 of *Briefe*, Rudolf Steiner Verlag, Dornach, 1953.
48 The Story of the Acts of the Apostles 2:2–3. The 'rushing of the wind' is a picture for spirit in its activity. See also the memorable conversation with Nicodemus (John 3:1–8), where the blowing of the wind and of the spirit is expressly mentioned in connection with a new birth.
49 Matthew 1:18.
50 Questions connected with the figures of Mary and Jesus in the Gospels of Matthew and Luke are very multi-layered, and a detailed description of this would be beyond the limits of this work. See therefore Rudolf Steiner, Notes 9 and 4, and *The Gospel of St John and its Relation to the Other Gospels*, Anthroposophic Press 1982. See also Note 47. In *Kindheit und Jugend Jesu* (Jesus' Childhood and Youth), Stuttgart 1988, Emil Bock gives a full presentation of these matters.
51 In *Die Christengemeinschaft*, December 1963, 'Das Mariengeheimnis—geistig, seelisch, leiblich' (The Mary Mystery from the Aspects of Spirit, Soul and Body). Three further essays bearing the same title, in other places, January, February and March 1964.
52 See Emil Bock's summary in *Kindheit und Jugend Jesu* (Jesus' Childhood and Youth), chapter on the great drama of Mary.
53 Book III, pp.77–78. Quoted from Wolfram von Eschenbach's

Parzival, translated by Helen M. Mustard and Charles E. Passage, Vintage Books, New York. For further aspects of this encounter, see Walter Schafarschik, *Wolfram von Eschenbach*, Salzburg 1983, p.106 and following.

54   See Walter Johannes Stein, *The Ninth Century, World History in the Light of the Holy Grail*, Temple Lodge Press, London 1991; Rudolf Meyer, *Zum Raum wird hier die Zeit* (Time Becomes Space), Stuttgart 1980.

55   See Note 53, Book V, p.129.

56   See Note 53, Book V, p.130.

57   Book IX, pp.251–52.

58   Book XVI, pp.414–45.

59   Rudolf Steiner, 'The Mysteries of the Orient and of Christianity'. Lecture of 7 February 1913 in Berlin. The Grail impulse can manifest in various forms. When they are genuine pictures they all lead to the Christ-Sophia Mystery. See also Mario Betti, *Wer ist der Gral?* (Who is the Grail?), Stuttgart 1984.

60   Rudolf Steiner, *Christ and the Spiritual World and the Search for the Holy Grail*, Rudolf Steiner Press 1983. Lecture of 1 January 1914, in Leipzig.

61   Ibid., lecture of 2 January 1914, in Leipzig.

62   Rudolf Steiner, *Macrocosm and Microcosm*, op. cit., and in other places. Lecture of 29 March 1910, in Vienna.

63   See Rudolf Meyer, *Zum Raum wird hier die Zeit* (Time Becomes Space), the chapter 'Im Zeichen des Rosenkreuzes' (In the Sign of the Rose Cross). Also George Adams, *Mysteries of the Rose Cross*, Temple Lodge Press, London 1989.

64   See *Anthroposophical Leading Thoughts*. Thought No 1.

65   Regarding these words of Wolfram von Eschenbach, see Walter Johannes Stein, *The Ninth Century. World History in the Light of the Holy Grail*, Temple Lodge Press, London 1991, p.94.

66   Rudolf Steiner, *The Search for the New Isis, the Divine Sophia*, Mercury Press, New York 1983. Lecture 25 December 1920 in Dornach.

67   Regarding these problems, see also Rainer Patzlaff, *Bildschirmtechnik und Bewusstseinsmanipulation* (Projection Technology and the Manipulation of Consciousness), Stuttgart 1987, chapter on the spiritual background to modern technology of projection; also Anton Kimpfler, *Die elektronische*

NOTES 91

Seuche (The Electronic Epidemic), Oberwil near Zug 1985, chapter on the TV habit and its consequences.

68 Marshall McLuhan, *Understanding Media*, Routledge and Kegan Paul, London 1984.

69 Ibid.

70 Quoted from Neil Postman, *The Disappearance of Childhood*, W.H. Allen, London 1983.

71 Rudolf Steiner, *Stages of Higher Knowledge*, op. cit. Lecture of 11 September 1920 in Dornach. The following quotations came from this lecture.

72 This means the soul in a comprehensive sense. See Rudolf Steiner, *Occult Science, An Outline*, op. cit., the chapter 'The Nature of Humanity'.

73 Ibid., the chapter 'Present and Future Evolution of the World and of Mankind'.

74 See the first chapter of the present book.

75 These are the words of a being who sponsored the Findhorn Movement. They were disclosed by its spiritual inaugurator. Quoted from Paul Hawken, *The Magic of Findhorn*, Souvenir Press, London 1975, pp.99–100.

76 See *Info 3*, Frankfurt a.M., September 1982, p.10. Also Lorenzo Ravagli, 'New Age—Aufbruch oder Schiffbruch' (Sink or Swim), in: *Die Kommenden*, Schaffhausen, May 1990.

77 Chris Griscom, *Zeit ist eine Illusion* (Time is an Illusion), Munich 1989, the chapter on the forging of energies.

78 Here, too, there is an abundance of literature giving practical guidance. See among other things Reinhard Fischer, *Raumfahrt der Seele—Erlebnisse im Umkreis der Mentalprojektion* (Space Travel of the Soul—Experiences in the Realm of Mental Projection), Freiburg i. Br., 1975; Robert A. Monroe, *Der Mann mit den zwei Leben—Reisen ausserhalb des Körpers* (The Man with Two Lives—Journeys Outside the Body), Interlaken 1981.

79 Ephesians 6:12.

80 See Hans-Werner Schroeder, *Der Mensch und das Böse* (Man and Evil), Stuttgart 1984.

81 Rudolf Steiner, *Die Brücke zwischen Weltgeistigkeit und dem Physischen des Menschen* (The Bridge Between Universal Spirituality and the Physical Constitution of Man), GA 202, Rudolf Steiner Verlag, Dornach. Lecture of 28 November 1920 in Dornach.

82   See Rudolf Steiner, *The Search for the New Isis, the Divine Sophia*, op. cit. Lecture of 24 December 1920 in Dornach. These words emphasize the *actual* character of the connections in question. Christ-Sophia experiences are at the same time seeds of the sixth cultural epoch, the epoch of the Spirit Self evolution. Regarding this aspect, see also the book by Sergei O. Prokofieff, *Eternal Individuality—Towards a Karmic Biography of Novalis*, Temple Lodge Publishing 1992 (especially the chapter 'Christ and Sophia'—The Mysteries of the Sixth Cultural Epoch).

83   Rudolf Steiner, *The Reappearance of Christ in the Etheric*, Anthroposophic Press 1983.

84   Ibid., lecture of 25 January 1910 in Karlsruhe.

85   Revelation of St John 21 and following.

86   Revelation of St John 12, 13–17.

87   To further deepen the pictures of the Apocalypse, see Rudolf Steiner, *The Apocalypse of St John*, Rudolf Steiner Press 1985. Also Emil Bock, *Apocalypse of St John*, Floris Books, Edinburgh 1986.

88   Regarding the 'lotus flowers' as higher organs of knowledge, see Rudolf Steiner, *Knowledge of the Higher Worlds. How is it Achieved?*, op. cit., chapter: 'Some Effects of Initiation'.

89   See Note 86.

90   Regarding Michael's activity, see Rudolf Steiner, *The Mission of the Archangel Michael*, Anthroposophic Press 1994. Also George Adams, *Mysteries of the Rose Cross* (second part), Temple Lodge Press 1989. In this study Adams points to the connection between Michael and imaginative consciousness.

91   See the essays by Sigismund von Gleich, in *Blätter für Anthroposophie*, No. 1.

92   See Herbert Wimbauer, *Jungfrau Sophia und ihr kosmisches Gegenbild* (The Virgin Sophia and her Cosmic Counter-image), Bollschweil 1981. This contains further important aspects of our theme.

93   *Parzival*, Books IV and XVI.

94   See Note 1.

95   See among other things L.F.C. Mees, *Rauschmittel—Warum?* (Drugs—Why?), Stuttgart 1975.

96   Rudolf Steiner, *The Effects of Spiritual Development*, Rudolf Steiner Press 1978. Lecture of 20 March 1913 at the Hague.

97   Revelation of St John 17, 1–15.